Getting Things Done

An Achiever's Guide to Time Management

By Paul Kraly
and
Paula Kalamaras
Edited by National Press Publications

NATIONAL PRESS PUBLICATIONS

A Division of Rockhurst College Continuing Education Center, Inc.
6901 West 63rd Street • P.O. Box 2949 • Shawnee Mission, Kansas 66201-1349
1-800-258-7248 • 1-913-432-7757

National Press Publications endorses nonsexist language. In an effort to make this handbook clear, consistent and easy to read, we've used "he" throughout the odd-numbered chapters, and "she" throughout the even-numbered chapters. The copy is not intended to be sexist.

Getting Things Done

Published by National Press Publications, Inc.
Copyright 1998 National Press Publications, Inc.
A Division of Rockhurst College Continuing Education Center, Inc.

Printed in the United States of America

13 14 15 16 17 18 19 20

ISBN 1-55852-012-0

Table of Contents

Introduction: Using Time..1

1   Self-Assessment, Goal Setting and Establishing Priorities...................5

2   Using Time at the Office: External Distractions 13

3   The Office: Organizing Techniques...31

4   The Office: Working With Others 43

5   The Office: Controlling Your Time 53

6   The Office: Crisis Time Management 63

7   Home: Time Planning for Working Parents 73

8   Home: Organizing...81

9   Stand By for Mind Control..91

10 Tips, Strategies and Timesaving Techniques.....................................103

Index..113

INTRODUCTION: USING TIME

"Time keeps on slipping...into the future"
— Steve Miller Band in "Fly Like an Eagle"

Why Do We Want to Save Time?

There's just so much time in a day, a month or a life. If you examine your use of time closely, you will find that you don't get things done because you waste valuable time each day.

Time is defined as a "nonspatial continuum in which events occur in apparently irreversible succession from the past through the present to the future." While we act as if we have all the time in the world, we complain we never have enough of it. You can't stop it or put it in a bottle. It flows with no consideration of what we want to do with it. Like "ole man river," it just keeps rolling along. Maybe you can't change the flow, but you can change the way you use it.

Using time falls into two categories: using it up or using it wisely. This book discusses the uses of time and offers tips and techniques to use it wisely at work and at home.

For example, you need to get a report done by the end of the day in order to attend your child's recital that evening. You work like crazy, running around like a chicken with its head cut off, trying at the last minute to organize the details that should have been done before. You're in a sweat that the job has not been done as well as it could have been. You run from your office, jump in your car and it doesn't start because you left the lights on all day. You finally get a jump start, race to the recital and find your child taking a final bow. What did you accomplish?

You are nervous, harried, worried, disheveled and in trouble at work and at home. How can you prevent this from happening again?

GET ORGANIZED!

Learn to manage the tasks, and learn to manage time.

Organization keeps your goals in focus and your life in order. The key to getting things done and using your time effectively is to organize yourself and your surroundings. Show the people around you how to organize too and you will find that you have much more time to get things done!

What's in This Handbook?

Effective time management means you decide what you need or want to get done and allot a realistic amount of time to complete the task. Squeezing too many activities into too short a time only leads to mistakes and chaos. Going to your child's recital would have been different if planned properly, allowing you to finish your report earlier in the week.

For some people, time management is a survival exercise. They live from crisis to crisis, always trying to survive the next deadline, hoping they won't drop the ball on the other projects they're juggling. People locked in the survival mode have trouble getting work done and then often blame it on poor time management. Not so—they cannot allocate their time properly. Time management and time allocation are separate issues and are easily confused.

Time management applies a predetermined group of guidelines to structure time spent on activities efficiently. Time allocation means making decisions and establishing priorities as a basis for deciding which tasks you will do and the sequence in which you will do them.

This handbook teaches strategies to organize your life and get things done. It helps you define what you want to do based on your own work style. You will learn to define your priorities and use them as a framework for time allocation decisions and find tips to organize your home and office with the tools you need to accomplish your goals. You'll learn to combine time management and time allocation skills to make you more efficient in specific situations at work and in your personal life.

Being in Control

Getting organized and using time effectively is up to you! This book puts you on track so you control time and events instead of letting them control you.

1 SELF-ASSESSMENT, GOAL SETTING AND ESTABLISHING PRIORITIES

Before you can achieve anything in life — big or small — you need to have a good idea of:

- Your style of work

- What you need to accomplish

- How and in what order you are going to get your tasks done

Everyone needs long- and short-term goals at the office, at home and for themselves. Without goals you live "reactively," where your decisions and actions are driven and determined solely by external forces, instead of "proactively," where your actions are driven by your priorities and goals. Living reactively can have negative consequences in your life — from affecting your career goals to determining what direction your life will take. Proactive planning and organizing gives you a clear and concise picture of your personal or career "road map."

If you are like most people, you have a long list of goals — far too many to reasonably achieve all at once. This is where setting priorities comes in handy. Priorities allow you to define a workable schedule for reaching your goals. However, make certain you establish a time frame for each to ensure you achieve your goals and priorities in a timely manner.

This road map tells you where you want to be and how to get there. But before we can really get into the specifics of creating your career, home and personal road maps, let's take a few moments to determine what your opinion of yourself in regard to work, home and self is at this point.

Establishing Goals

The first step to organizing your work, home and personal life is to set your goals. Without goals, you can spend huge amounts of time on things that are of little or no importance to you. As a result, you never accomplish the things you really want to do! Instead, you spend too much time spinning your wheels in an endless circle of doing everything but what you want to do.

This sounds very nice, you say. Then how do you establish the goals? It's really very easy. First, get a sheet of paper and a pencil (or if you are high tech, a blank page on your computer's word processor). Then sit down for 15 to 20 minutes with the express purpose of setting a series of goals.

Ask yourself what you want to do in your personal life, at your job and in your home. Then begin by using active, action-oriented words to record what it is that you want. Are you interested in becoming a professional musician? Do you want to take a family vacation? Lose 25 pounds? Become a vice president of your company? Run for public office?

When you are setting your goals, consider these questions:

1. **What do I want from my job?**

2. **What do I want to accomplish at home?**

3. **What do I want to do for myself?**

Now examine this list and ask yourself the following questions about the goals you've established:

- Is this something I really want?

- Am I willing to do what is necessary to achieve this goal?

- Do I have the skills to meet this goal?

Let's say that your goal has always been to be a professional musician. When you ask yourself if this is something that you really want, your answer should be a resounding yes! However, when you ask yourself if you are willing to do what is necessary to achieve this goal, you have to honestly answer practicing was never your thing and in fact, you haven't picked up an instrument in years for serious practice.

You can safely take this goal off your active goal list and set it into the "daydream list." This doesn't mean that if you do acquire the skills and the dedication to become a musician that you can't reactivate this goal.

In setting goals, keep the following guidelines in mind:

- Make goals specific and measurable.

  A vague statement such as "I want to make more money" is not measurable. If you say, "I want to increase my current salary by at least 20 percent in the next two years," then you have defined a specific goal.

- Be flexible.

  Just as your life changes, so will your goals. Review them often to see if they are still relevant to your needs and interests. Take your goal to be a professional musician for example. That may have been your goal when you were 16 years old. When you review that goal at 25, you find that your life has gone in an entirely different direction. While this may have been a worthy goal in your youth, your needs have changed and so too have your goals.

- Put your goals in writing.

  Writing down goals makes them more concrete. Don't fall into the trap of thinking that just because they are in writing, you don't have to think about them, though! Review them often. Keep a copy with you at all times.

How many times have you made a New Year's resolution, told a few people about it and then within days forgotten it as if it had never been? How different would it be if that resolution was put in writing and kept where you could see it regularly? Think about it when you make your next year's resolutions.

- Break big goals into smaller ones.

This simple trick will keep your goals more manageable and less threatening. Suppose your goal is to become the president of your company and you are currently a supervisor. You will need to create sub-goals that will help you achieve your ultimate goal. For instance, in two years, you want to become a manager trainee, then a manager within four years, and so on. You may not achieve the ultimate goal, but you have set up an advancement plan.

Breaking down your goals into sub-goals can assist you on the home and personal fronts as well. Let's say you want to buy a house. It costs $150,000. You could set your goal to be "I will pay for this house in ten years." Your sub-goals would then be:

- Saving the down payment

- Making certain that you find the best rates and secure financing

- Working for each month's mortgage payment, etc.

- Cross off your goals when you accomplish them.

The very act of crossing off your goals when you reach them gives you a sense of accomplishment. It helps you keep track of your progress. It also encourages you to record your next goal, once you actually see the results of the ones you have already completed.

Write down five of your primary goals and list the sub-goals for each. Refer to the example for buying a house.

Goal 1: _____

    Sub-goals: _____

    _____

    _____

    _____

Goal 2: _____

    Sub-goals: _____

    _____

    _____

    _____

Goal 3: _____

    Sub-goals: _____

    _____

    _____

    _____

Goal 4: _____

    Sub-goals: _____

    _____

    _____

    _____

Goal 5: _____

    Sub-goals: _____

    _____

    _____

    _____

Reflections

Setting and Adhering to Priorities

Priorities define those things in life that are important to you. They may be pressing tasks for work, personal obligations, activities that bring personal fulfillment or decisions dictated by your values. So the first step is to establish your goals and then to prioritize them. Decide what is important to you and in what order. Take a moment to jot this down, being sure to include personal, career and family priorities.

Knowing what your priorities are and sticking to them are very different things. Because you always have a lot of responsibilities at work, at home and to yourself, you may find that you are being pulled in several different directions. If you are not careful, you may find that your own priorities are being delegated to the back burner or that several priorities may conflict with one another. If this is the case, reassess your priorities and make certain that they are not in conflict. Ask yourself the following questions:

- How does this project, request, etc., fit in with my priorities?

- Is it appropriate for me to assume responsibility for this task? Can I say "no" without jeopardizing my job, home or sanity?

- What impact will diverting my time have on accomplishing other tasks? Meeting other deadlines?

- Can this task be done or solved by others? If so, by whom?

In order to stick to your own priorities, make certain that they are at the forefront of your mind. Even if situations arise that challenge or threaten to disrupt your time, always keep your goals and priorities in focus. If you have a developed plan, then even interruptions won't let you stray too far from it.

Developing a Plan of Action

Once you set the goals and establish the priority to pursue them, it is time for you to start working on a plan of action to help you accomplish these goals. A plan of action outlines how you intend to achieve your goal and establishes a deadline to complete it.

Let's go back to the goal of "taking a family vacation." You need to plan for the following:

- How much will the vacation cost?

- How do you intend to save money for it?

- How are you going to get the money? Can you put away $100 per paycheck for the next 6 months?

- Will you need another source of income?

Now establish a deadline because that will help you avoid the trap of procrastination.

Write out this plan and then set your deadlines and monetary goals on a calendar. This way, you will have a written record of your accomplishments and be able to see at a glance where you stand.

Goal: To save $1,200 by July 15

How will this be done? Paychecks are on the first and fifteenth of each month. Beginning January 1, I will save a minimum of $100 per paycheck. In six months, I will have the $1,200 — the amount I need to take that family vacation!

See how setting goals, establishing priorities and developing a plan of action will let you achieve those things that you really want in life?

Using three of your goals from the previous reflection, list each goal and write down your plan of action for each one. Include a deadline date for completion. Use the example of saving $1,200 by July 15 to help you get started.

Goal 1: _____

    Plan of action: _____

    _____

    _____

    Deadline for completion: _____

Goal 2: _____

    Plan of action: _____

    _____

    _____

    Deadline for completion: _____

Goal 3: _____

    Plan of action: _____

    _____

    _____

    Deadline for completion: _____

Reflections

2 USING TIME AT THE OFFICE: EXTERNAL DISTRACTIONS

Throughout your work day, you have to deal with situations that take you away from the work you are assigned to finish. There are many interruptions: meetings, phone calls, visitors. Each one of these events, as well as the accompanying social interactions, creates distractions. Sometimes they are necessary and vital to the flow of work at the office or even for the completion of your projects. But this doesn't mean you just let them happen! It is very important to get these typical time-wasters under control and move them back into the realm where they help you and not hurt you in achieving your goals and priorities. Let's look at these three major distractors, beginning with meetings.

Meetings

Meetings consume high amounts of time for everyone, and little of it is constructive time. The key to a successful meeting is organization. Whether it is a large or small, meetings provide exclusive time to exchange information and make decisions about a common goal. So whatever you do, make certain that you plan your meeting with the understanding that you are gathering to get something done. If you find yourself attending too many meetings where you are not making a contribution or gathering important information, reassess whether you should even be going. Unorganized meetings destroy the best time management plans.

Pre-Meeting Organization

The first thing you must ask yourself is, "Is a meeting necessary, or can I communicate this issue through other means?" If the answer is no or it is important that you have the input of other persons, then you have to have a meeting.

Whatever you do, don't just call the meeting without planning or all you'll get is a scattered and disorganized event that takes far too much time.

During pre-planning, ask yourself these questions (in writing):

- What do you want to achieve by holding this meeting?

- What topics need discussion?

- Who has the information/knowledge that is crucial to these topics and objectives?

The answers to these questions will provide the framework for an effective agenda, identify the people to invite and help you estimate how much time you should budget for the meeting.

During your pre-planning, remember that most people "zone out" and stop hearing what you have to say if a meeting is over an hour long. There is only so much time that you can discuss a topic without repeating yourself. Try to keep meetings short and to the point!

This is not to say that all meetings should be limited, but that depends on the topic and how much has to be done. For the most part, 60 minutes should enable you to get the information and the input you need to move on to the next task.

Create Your Agenda Early

Structuring the meeting, an agenda helps you keep control of the event as well as lets the participants know what aspects of a topic are to be discussed.

The agenda should support your meeting objectives by including time for discussion of the topics and issues that must be resolved in order for your objectives (and the purpose of the meeting) to be met. When structuring the agenda, include specific opportunities to:

- State the purpose of the meeting.

- Summarize the key issues and the overall discussion.

- Reach conclusions.

- Identify responsibilities for assigned tasks.

Create a Checklist

One of the keys to organizing a meeting is preparing a checklist. This will alleviate the problems of the planning because it asks the questions that focus your attention on the details and gives you the advantage of having a list in hand. These checklists take the logistics of the meeting plan and organize it, leaving you free to worry about the substance of the meeting.

Here is a sample checklist that can assist you in organizing your next meeting:

Sample checklist

I. Pre-Meeting Planning

Name of group or meeting:_____

Topic: _____

Date of meeting: _____

Time of meeting:_____

Location of meeting:_____

Is it necessary to reserve the location? Yes ❒   No ❒

Who will reserve the room? _____

Date done: _____

Names of persons to attend meeting (attach list)

Who will issue invitations?_____

How will the invitations be issued?   Letter ❒

    Phone call ❒   Interoffice memo ❒   Personal visit ❒

    Number of responses: _____

Will refreshments be served?   Yes ❒   No ❒

    If no, go on to the next section; if yes, please continue:

What will be served? _____

_____

_____

Who will pick up and deliver? _____

_____

Has this person been notified of the task? When? _____

II. Room Setup

How big is the room? How many persons can be seated comfortably?

_____

_____

Who is responsible for setup? Has this person been notified? How?

_____

Are there special equipment requirements needed for the meeting?

_____

Have you notified the appropriate support persons (a/v crew, maintenance crew, etc.)?   Yes ☐   No ☐

Audio visual?   Yes ☐   No ☐

    Overhead projector? Yes ☐   No ☐

        Where is it? _____

        Is it working? Yes ☐   No ☐

        Transparencies? Are they complete? Yes ☐   No ☐

    Slide projector?   Yes ☐   No ☐

        Where is it? _____

        Does it work?   Yes ☐   No ☐

    Screen?   Yes ☐   No ☐

        Who has it? _____

        Who sets it up? _____

    TV-VCR?   Yes ☐   No ☐

        Is it reserved and ready for use?   Yes ☐   No ☐

        Are the tapes ready?   Yes ☐   No ☐

        Who has them? _____

        Who will bring them to the meeting? _____

Video camera?　　Yes ❑　　　No ❑

　　Who will operate? _____

　　Do you have enough tape and supplies? Yes ❑　No ❑

　　Is it necessary?　　Yes ❑　　　No ❑

Easel pad and marking pens/black board?　Yes ❑　　No ❑

　　Where are they? _____

　　Who will bring them? _____

Paper and pens for participants?　　Yes ❑　　No ❑

Do you need an extension cord? Where is it?

Yes ❑　No ❑　　_____

Do you have extra bulbs and incidentals to ensure that the equipment works?　Yes ❑　No ❑

If you are having refreshments, where are you setting them?

_____

Agenda?　　Yes ❑　No ❑

　Who has the agenda? _____

　Are there handouts?　　Yes ❑　　No ❑

　Do you have enough copies of each?　　Yes ❑　　No ❑

　Who sets them out? _____

Do you need name tags?　Yes ❑　　No ❑

III. Meeting

Who will run the meeting? _____

How long will the meeting last? _____

Who controls the meeting? _____

How will the proceedings be recorded? _____

Who is responsible for the minutes? _____

Do you have a backup person for notes available? _____

Deadlines: who sets them and when are they? _____

IV. Post-meeting assessment

Who cleans up? _____

Who issues notes and minutes and sends to participants? _____

Who monitors that this is done? _____

This checklist is very useful for setting up a meeting with a minimum of fuss. Of course, like every list, all the items are not necessarily applicable to you and your meetings.

Once you have your external logistics set, it's time for you to begin planning the substance of the meeting.

Who Attends the Meeting?

The more people who attend a meeting, the less productive the meeting becomes and the more time it takes. So it is up to you to limit the number of persons who are actually involved. You can always inform others of the results later via memo or a phone call.

Limit attendance to persons who have the greatest amount of information, knowledge or expertise that is essential to discussing the issues, and are necessary to make decisions. The best use of your time is ensured if you make certain that those who will implement tasks are in attendance! It is also vital that attendance be limited to the persons who will be responsible for the follow-up activities. If you ask too many people to attend, a clear line of authority is blurred and persons who are necessary to follow-up the assignments may receive conflicting messages as to what they are supposed to do.

When you invite persons to attend a meeting:

- Define the purpose.

- Give them as much background information as possible.

- Indicate at the outset what you hope to accomplish.

- Summarize why they are being asked to attend and what you expect of them.

- Indicate that the meeting will begin promptly at a specific time and how long it will last.

When you contact these persons, either by memo or call, make certain that they know why they are being included in the meeting. Often there are times when some individuals may fall into a gray area and could or could not be included. Try to identify in your own mind whether their contribution is necessary or whether they merely need to be kept informed. If at a later time you find that you should have included a person, set aside time to meet privately, bring them up to speed and make certain that they are on all future invitation lists.

Controlling the Meeting

Control of a meeting starts when you decide to hold it, not the minute you call it to order. It requires a clear understanding of the purpose of the meeting and what you want to accomplish. In short, just as you set goals for yourself, you have to have goals for the meeting. Don't schedule a meeting unless you are very clear on these points.

You control the meeting before it starts by your choice of participants, the location, the time and the length of the meeting. Controlling factors include:

- Introducing the purpose of the meeting.

- Providing a brief outline of the purpose of the meeting in your opening remarks. Tell everyone what you want to accomplish. Discuss the ground rules that you want to follow. (And follow them!)

- Acting as a referee for the differing points of view. You must keep reminding the group of the purpose for the meeting in order to get the discussion back on track.

- Guiding the group toward consensus and conclusions.

- Summarizing decisions that are made, identifying responsibilities and deadlines.

After the meeting is concluded, continue control by managing the follow-up process:

- Write (or have transcribed) the agreed-upon tasks, responsibilities and deadlines and distribute them to all participants.

- Establish checkpoints to monitor the progress.

- Monitor deadlines and make certain that they are reached.

Meeting Reports

A report should go to each participant to summarize the discussion and decisions that were made. Also send a copy of the report to the people who need to be aware of the proceedings of the meeting but who did not attend.

The report should include:

- Summary of each discussion item.

- Indication of any tasks that were assigned.

- Indication of who is responsible for implementation.

- Outline of the deadlines/budgets that were established.

Avoid the Unproductive Meeting!

Don't waste your time sitting in a meeting where you don't contribute. But how can you know if this is a meeting that you should avoid? Well, if you are specifically assigned to a meeting by your boss, you have to go without question. But if you have a choice and question whether you should attend, use these same sorts of techniques that helped you plan your own meeting in the first place.

- Determine the purpose of the meeting in advance.

- Establish the meeting's length (control how much time you can allocate by scheduling another commitment if you have to).

- Ask for an agenda.

Based on the above, decide whether your participation is essential. If not, gracefully suggest that you need not attend but that you are willing to discuss any questions or problems that the person calling the meeting might have. Offer your expertise, but not your valuable time.

Telephone Calls: Handling Calls Efficiently

The telephone is the second great interrupter and time waster. Picture this. You really need to concentrate on the task at hand. You are ready to start, your focus is set and then…the phone rings. Suddenly you are being controlled by the outside world. Make this stop by being in control of your telephone calls!

When you don't want to be interrupted, make the following arrangements:

- Have your calls held if you have a secretary or a switchboard. If you don't, disconnect the phone or use the "do not disturb" button if there is one.

- If you can't disconnect but you can forward your calls, make arrangements with a colleague.

These simple solutions will help you control your time and to whom you speak during the day. If you are taking calls but want to limit your conversations, let the caller know at the start of the call that there is a time limit on your conversation. You only have so much time to talk. Make certain that you cut the small talk and focus on the issues at hand. Ask specific questions that require the caller to identify the purpose of the call and what is needed from you. When you are nearing the end of the allocated time, inform the caller that time is about up and wrap up the conversation.

When you are the caller, organize your thoughts ahead of time. Write a little outline of the points you want to cover and stick to them. Avoid idle chit-chat. Save that for when you both have the time. Make sure you get right to the point, and if the conversation gets long-winded, tell the other party you have another call or someone has walked into the office. A great deal of time is wasted by not organizing the time you spend initiating phone calls. This process involves setting priorities.

The key to getting your calls organized is to place calls of like type in similar priority groups. Obviously, calls that must be returned or made immediately can't be postponed. Other calls, on the other hand, can be delayed. These guidelines offer effective and timesaving organization in your call returns:

- Arrange calls that need to be returned or initiated into priority groups.

- Budget a block of time to make all the calls in the highest-priority group.

- Schedule time throughout the day to make the calls in the other groups.

- Budget the time for them during the parts of the day that are typically unproductive. Some of these include:

  1. Waiting for a visitor to arrive in your office.

  2. Waiting for a meeting to begin.

  3. During a low energy level period (late afternoon, after lunch).

  4. Other predictable blocks of idle time.

If you need additional time to make telephone calls, set aside 15- to 30-minute periods during natural breaking points: just before lunch, 30 minutes before you go home, at break time and so on. Avoid fragmenting your time by not making calls outside of the scheduled periods if possible.

Drop-In Visitors

You want to have an open-door policy, but you still want to have the time to finish all of your work. You want your staff to have access to you, but you don't want to be interrupted by casual drop-in visitors. You can do this and still get your work done. Just follow a few of these simple suggestions:

Drop-ins

Establish periods each day when your door is "open" to drop-in visitors. Depending on your needs, this can be once or twice a day.

Communicate to staff and colleagues what the schedule is for these drop-ins. Stress that if it is a dire emergency — not merely a problem — you can be interrupted.

Unannounced visitors

If an unannounced visitor turns up in your office despite these efforts, stand up immediately and don't invite the person to sit down. Ask the visitor to describe the emergency. This conveys that you are being interrupted and discourages casual conversation.

Making appointments

Encourage staff and colleagues to make appointments to discuss problems or questions that they have. This encourages them to organize their thoughts before they meet with you or try to solve the problem themselves. Also encourage subordinates to compile a list of questions they need to ask you and present them all at once instead of interrupting you several times.

It's Friday afternoon and you are in the middle of a major project that has to be done by the end of the day. You have arranged to have all of your calls held by your assistant. You are planning to return them at the end of the work day, after you have finished your project. All of a sudden, you are interrupted by a co-worker who wants to chat about an unrelated issue. You need to work with this person on a regular basis. How do you handle this situation? What actions do you take?

_____

_____

_____

Your boss interrupts you next to check on your progress with the project and doesn't seem as if she is planning to leave. What do you do in this situation?

_____

_____

_____

Your assistant believes that there is an emergency that can only be handled by you. How do you determine whether this is the case? What questions do you ask?

_____

_____

_____

What can you do to avoid unneeded interruptions?

_____

_____

_____

Reflections

Use Time Efficiently

Anticipate occasions when you have idle time. These times include waiting for meetings to begin or visitors to arrive, traveling, waiting for a telephone call, waiting at a doctor's office, etc. Use this time to your advantage.

- Return/make low-priority phone calls.

- Dictate routine memos or correspondence.

- Sort and read your mail.

- Scan magazines and less-urgent correspondence, professional journals, etc.

- Use this time to build relationships with vendors and clients through phone calls, letters, greeting cards, etc.

Make More Time for Yourself

If you are a manager or your job requires a lot of interaction with others, you may find it hard to get the quiet time you need to get your assigned tasks accomplished. If you have to frequently leave the office frustrated because you can't find the time to do certain things, consider coming in early or staying late.

Many busy executives arrive at their offices ahead of other employees or stay one or two hours late to give themselves the time to get their paperwork and other undelegatable routine tasks done. Be careful, however, not to let this turn into wasted time. If others have the same idea, you may find yourselves drinking coffee and talking instead of getting work done. This is not the best way to use time. If this becomes the case, you may as well go back to coming in on time and working throughout the day.

Another way is to set aside the first half hour of each day to work on the routine tasks. Get these done, answer phone calls and such and you will find that your day is more easily managed. Don't reinvent the wheel.

Don't start from scratch every time you write a letter or a report. Always check to see if there are other portions of your work that you can reuse.

If you send several letters to many people that, for example, review what was discussed in a conference or meeting last week, a few changes with the word processor allows you to send the same letter to everyone who needs it. If your boss asks for a report that is similar to another you have done, look back to see what changes have been made to the earlier report and use the time to make those changes to the present report. For this reason, it is very important to keep a record of the work you do either on computer disk or similar storage capacities. Think of the time you will save!

Be Flexible

You arrive at the office raring to go on your day's planned activities. As soon as you arrive, your boss sidetracks you onto another assignment. You were all set to work on the speech for the annual luncheon and now you are suddenly working on a piece of legislation to be presented to council.

Sometimes no matter how carefully you plan your time and focus your priorities, something else comes along that is more important, supersedes your efforts and gets you onto a different track. Don't panic. One of the great keys to using time wisely is learning to cope with these times by anticipating that they will happen. Stay cool and follow a few steps to make it through the change in plans.

Take a deep breath and relax

Getting angry or anxious won't help. If you can, go to your office and close the door. Take a few deep breaths and count to 100. Think things through. Then go out and get the job done.

Consider your options

If you work on the new project today, figure out when you will be able to work on the original project later in the week. Can you meet the deadline on either project? Is there someone in the office who can assist you in completing these two projects. Can you delegate it to him?

Learn to juggle

Look at your calendar and see what can be rescheduled. What can you change to give you the time you need to complete the project? If necessary, cancel meetings, lunches or other things of lower priority.

Ask for help

If you don't think you can complete both projects, don't hesitate to ask for help. It could yield a new deadline, extend the time for your projects and offer you reasonable alternatives. Your boss may not realize the commitments that you have and can release other resources for both of you.

Using the form below, determine how your day is spent. What type of distractions keep you from your assigned tasks and how can you handle them?

Time	Task	Deadline	Interruptions	Solutions
6:00				
6:30				
7:00				
7:30				
8:00				
8:30				
9:00				
9:30				
10:00				
10:30				
11:00				
11:30				
Noon				
12:30				
1:00				
1:30				
2:00				
2:30				
3:00				
3:30				
4:00				
4:30				
5:00				
5:30				
6:00				

Reflections

3 THE OFFICE: ORGANIZING TECHNIQUES

Have you ever had your boss come in and request a report or letter that was given to you? You are on the phone, the boss is standing in the doorway and there on your desk are three or four one-foot-high piles of paper. You ask your caller to hold a second, even though it's an important call. You begin frantically searching through the piles for the item the boss wants. The boss stands there tapping his fingers impatiently. The caller is trying to get your attention and you can't find the paper the boss needs.

Finally, in desperation, you tell the boss that you will bring it to him in five minutes. He walks away, upset that you cannot seem to handle even a simple request. The caller is upset that you were so rude as to interrupt an important call. You are upset because you feel you failed on all fronts. You hurriedly finish the conversation feeling you shortchanged the caller. You frantically search through the piles of paper that you meant to sort, and there on the bottom of the last pile you find the report you need. You run with it breathless to your boss's office and hand it to him. He thanks you, but looks at you strangely and suggests that you need to "get organized."

The boss is right. You do. Do you find yourself moving this paper to that pile, moving that paper to that folder or searching frantically for something that "was right here"? It's called the paper shuffle. It's a great waste of time and effort because when you are done shuffling the papers, you are no further ahead than when you started. In fact, sometimes you're worse off because you are frazzled and stressed at not finding what you need.

Suppose the scene with your boss had been played differently. Your boss comes to your office and you are on the phone. He excuses himself and asks for a report that he gave you but now needs. You politely ask the caller to hold "just a second." You think for a moment about the report and realize that it is something that you were using a little while before. You look at the rack of folders that hold the current work, finger through the labels and get the report, handing it to the boss. You make a note of your actions so that you remember where the report is when you need it again. He thanks you cheerfully and goes on his way. You return to your call and complete it without a second thought and then move on to your next task (without taking time to windsprint with the document to your boss's office). Everyone is happy. No stress and no wasted time was spent searching for the report because of your splendid organizing skills.

You can clear your desk without giving the impression that you never work. Get a system that puts everything you need within easy access. This system enables you to keep on top of things and save valuable time to actually accomplish them because you won't be searching for them in a hurried frenzy.

Evaluate

Before you do anything else, you need to assess what is going on in your office. Do you have everything you need to get the job done? Do you have the right equipment and supplies? Do you have to run to the supply room every time you need a pen or a pad of paper? Are you always running out of computer diskettes?

While it may seem that these are trivial items to worry about when you have so much important work to do, the equipment and supplies you use and how you have them organized are keys to getting things done.

Desktop

Do you have papers scattered all over the top of your desk? Are they organized or do you have to hunt for each item every time you need it. If you can find the things you need in a matter of seconds, don't worry about what it looks like. Neatness doesn't count, organization does. On the other hand, if you have to spend a half an hour every time you want to find something, get a system — fast.

Put your projects in clearly visible, colored folders. For instance, you may assign red folders to jobs that have super priority, blue ones to long-term projects, yellow to phone messages and call follow-ups and green to letters and correspondence. For example, suppose you suddenly need to update a long-term project's status. Instead of searching through every folder and piece of paper on your desk, you concentrate your efforts on the blue ones. Within seconds you have your hands on the project that you need.

For some people, neatly labeled file folders in file cabinets is the most efficient way to organize the paperwork that crosses their desks. Some work best with piles that are stacked with similar documents. You have to find your own style of organization and do what is best for you. Just remember that the key isn't how you organize, but that you organize.

Around your desk

Examine the clutter on your desk. How is it arranged? Is your telephone in the most convenient spot? Does your computer really need to sit in the middle of the desk or would it be better if it were over to one side? Do you have all the things you use frequently within easy reach? Do you have all the supplies you need or are you constantly looking for a pencil or a pad of paper?

If, after answering these questions, you find that the items around your desk are not the ones that you need immediately, correct the situation. Once you have your desk arranged (and that includes inside the drawers too), you will save time because you will not be wasting motions. You won't have to get up to answer the phone because it's on a table across the room or move your computer to the side every time you need work space. When you run out of paper, you can open a desk drawer and get another pad, not run down the hall to the supply room. You will also know when to go to the supply room, since you will be able to see at a glance what and how much you need.

Inventory

Make out a small inventory of your office supplies and keep tabs on what you use and when. Once you start to run low, you can then take the time to go to the supply room, knowing exactly what you need and how much. Also make sure there is an inventory list for the supply room itself. Have you ever gone to the supply room only to find that your office is completely out of notepads? An item list inside the cabinet door, with appropriate marks and dates, can ensure your supply meets the demand.

Phone directory

How do you record your phone numbers? Do you have a phone directory or a card system? If you don't, get one. Record your most frequently called numbers in this directory or card system. Using the municipal phone book or calling information is a huge waste of time. Keeping often-called numbers handy saves time and frustration.

Don't plan to retype or recopy all of the numbers in your current directory into a new one. Starting now, do a new card every time you call someone or write the information in your directory. Before you know it, you will have a useable phone directory.

If typing cards is too much trouble, print the information. Print a number in pencil either on a card or in your phone book. That way you can change it if the number or address changes. If you have a computer, most programs offer you a card file or database option where you can store phone numbers. It only takes a few moments to add or change a number here, and then you can print out updated lists periodically if you don't want to look it up on-line each time you need a number. Many times the computer program has the ability to print out cards, so you may want to look into that option as well.

Or, set up a business card directory. Store each card you receive in a folder (there are many business card holders on the market) or make your own filing system.

Staple the business card to a 3×5 card and put it in a card file box with notes on the card relevant to your business. Or, place it in a notebook of similar cards. Do whatever works for you to help you access often-called numbers in an efficient and meaningful way.

Look at the top of your desk. Describe it.

_____

_____

_____

What can you do to organize it? What is your plan?

_____

_____

_____

Do you keep an accurate inventory of your office supplies? If not, create one. Decide where you will keep it for easy reference and updating.

_____

_____

_____

Do you have a phone directory? Do you frequently update it?

_____

_____

_____

How do you keep track of your most frequently called numbers?

_____

_____

_____

Reflections

Space

Do you have enough file space in your office or are your files stacked up on top and around the file cabinet? Are you using your computer and storage disks to their fullest capacity (and are you marking them)? You need to figure out why you have a filing problem. Do you keep too much nonessential information or do you simply have inadequate filing space in cabinets, on disks or on-line?

If the problem is nonessential material, start pitching. If it's inadequate space, lobby your boss for another file cabinet or a space in the office where you can store important but currently inactive files. If you need more storage on your computer, ask for more diskettes or more on-line memory to help you keep your files.

Whatever you need, once you organize your documents, you must be able to store them properly so you can retrieve them quickly and efficiently. Why color code your files only to pile them on the floor because you don't have a drawer available?

Time

Keep a calendar with adequate space to note appointments, important dates and deadlines. Do you have a calendar with adequate space to write down everything you need to do? Make certain you keep it handy so that when you note an appointment, it will be in the calendar and not on an easily lost scrap of paper.

Use the calendar on your computer to record your daily schedule. Print it and bring it with you. Store these in a notebook, and you will have a complete record of your activities.

Office equipment

Is the office equipment you use the best there is to get the job done? If not, what do you need that will?

Let's say that your job requires a monthly direct mail letter to be sent to your city's florists offering them specials on seasonal flowers. You only have an electric typewriter to complete the job. This means creating a form letter and then typing in all the addresses by hand. Not a great use of your time, is it?

Talk to your boss about a computer that will generate the letters in one-tenth of the time. Point out that you are not only helping yourself but the company as well. With the time you save, you will be able to search out and contact more markets for your floral products.

If the equipment is not in the budget, sell your idea to your boss. Research other computer products. When you present your idea, be ready to justify the cost of the equipment against what the company will ultimately save. Show the boss that by freeing you from typing letters, you will be able to devote more of your time to other more important tasks.

The Organizer

By organizing space and systems, you free your time to increase efficiency, which, in turn, increases productivity in your workplace. But don't stop there. Take your organizational skills with you wherever you go by making or purchasing an organizer. An organizer is a time management system designed to put everything you need right at your fingertips. It includes goal sheets, expense reports, a place to keep your receipts and much more. You can take notes, jot down ideas and make or change appointments anywhere. Addresses, phone numbers and business cards are immediately available right next to your monthly calendar.

Clearing the Paper Pileup

You don't have to put a match to your desk to cut down on the paperwork. Go through your desk and examine the papers. Don't just skim them and put them aside. Try the **TAF** system.

Decide to:

1. **T**hrow it away.

2. **A**ct on it.

3. **F**ile it.

Don't get caught in the "I'll need it someday" syndrome. An estimated 80 percent of the paper you receive can be thrown away. Whenever you feel like keeping a piece of paper, ask yourself the following questions:

1. **Will I use it?**

   If you don't know, throw it away.

2. **What will I use it for?**

   If you don't know, throw it away.

3. **When will I use it?**

   If you don't know, throw it away.

Avoid Future Pileups

Now that your paper pile is cleared away, keep it away. Follow these tips to keep paper on your desk at a minimum.

Use the TAF rule

When you go through your mail or in-basket, make an immediate decision about each piece of paper. Toss it, act on it or file it. Avoid putting it aside to deal with later.

Create your own personal reading file

Whenever you find an article you want to read, tear it out and put it in your reading file. Carry this file with you at all times. Read the articles while you are waiting for meetings or appointments to begin. This way you will use what would otherwise be "dead time" for something productive.

Review and re-evaluate your subscriptions and information that you routinely receive at the office

If you have piles of unread magazines, articles and newsletters stacking up, chances are that you can live without them. Evaluate what you really need and then cancel subscriptions that you don't. If you are getting papers, reports or other interoffice documents that are unnecessary to your job, ask to be taken off the routing list. You will be surprised at how much additional space you will acquire when you don't have these unnecessary items cluttering up your desk.

Limit trips

Don't waste time making trips to the copier or the mail room. Throughout the day, accumulate mail and papers needed to be copied. Then make one trip to the mail room and copy room on your way to lunch and again a few hours before leaving for the evening.

Now that you are clearing that clutter, how do you keep it down?

1. Look around your office. Do you need more filing space or do you need to organize the space you already have? What system do you use to file your papers away? Can it be improved?

    _____

    _____

2. How do you plan your day? Do you use a calendar with enough room to write down all of your tasks? Do you take an organizer with you to meetings and also use it at home? Do you transfer all planned events to your calendar to make certain that you have a handle on what you are doing?

    _____

    _____

3. Are you using the right equipment? Assess what other equipment you need to get the job done more efficiently. Is it possible for you to get it, and if not, what can you do to compensate?

    _____

    _____

4. How do you handle your mail? Do you use the TAF system? How often does your mail just sit until you throw it away without looking at it? What can you do to improve this? What time of day can you clear the clutter? What system can you use and what can you do to avoid future pileups?

    _____

    _____

5. How much time do you think it will take you to organize your office? Be honest.

    _____

    _____

Reflections

4 THE OFFICE: WORKING WITH OTHERS

In a perfect world, you might have total control of your time. But you are often dependent on others to help you get the job done.

Someone is usually in charge. If you are that person, here are some helpful tips to help you work with others to get things done without a lot of wasted time.

Explain What Needs to be Done

In simple, direct terms, state what needs to be accomplished. Don't vaguely say "you need to help me on this project." That doesn't tell your co-worker a thing. It's just a nebulous statement that says maybe sometime down the line, you might need assistance. This will not help you get the job done.

Instead, saying, "We need to work together to complete a marketing plan for a new bar of soap the company has created," communicates to the co-worker a good idea of the scope of the project.

Explain the co-worker's role in the overall completion of the project

In explaining exactly what you want your co-worker to do, you communicate the importance of the person's participation in the overall project. It inspires people to perform better when they understand that their role is vital.

Give your co-worker a time frame in which to work and estimate the amount of time needed to complete the project

Be fair. In order to work effectively, your co-worker needs to know how much time is needed to accomplish the assigned task. More importantly, the co-worker needs to know when it must be completed.

Be considerate

When you get a project, don't sit on it until the last minute and then expect others to drop their work to bail you out. Give your co-workers as much advance notice as possible.

Remember the "Golden Rule"

Treat others the way you would like to be treated. Saying "Please" and "Thank you" gains you more mileage than giving orders.

Remember the incentives and rewards

If there is a special incentive involved, share the information with your co-worker. Extra time off or a place on the promotion list might be the spur needed to inspire better performance.

Foster a spirit of cooperation

If several people must work together, stress teamwork and team spirit. Show you appreciate their efforts. It will go a long way in inspiring excellence.

Give credit

If it's appropriate, put your co-workers names on the project or report. If you can't do so, write memos thanking them for their help and explain how their assistance made it possible for the assignment to be completed on time. Remember to send a copy to your boss, the co-worker's boss and personnel.

Building Good Working Relationships

Good working relationships make your office a nicer place to spend your days and also assure you the assistance of your co-workers when you need it. Here are some tips on building good working relationships with your colleagues.

Get to know your fellow employees

Always greet your co-workers by name and learn a little bit about each of them. Are they married? Do they have children? Do they have special hobbies or interests? This gives you valuable clues to their behavior. You will know if sudden moodiness or inability to meet a deadline is usual or a result of outside stresses.

Be friendly

Overlook occasional outbursts

If a co-worker snaps at you or cuts you off occasionally, overlook it and work to mend any grievances between you. Hostility only breeds more hostility. If it happens frequently, however, find out why. You may need that co-worker's help.

You are in charge of a huge project that has been divided among five employees including yourself. The co-workers assigned to you are strangers. What steps do you take to create a genuine sense of teamwork? How do you encourage these strangers to work together to complete the project professionally and on time?

How do you explain how the components of the project interact?

_____

_____

What words do you use to explain the importance of your co-workers' role in the completion of the project?

_____

_____

How do you monitor the progress without intruding? What checkpoints have you set?

_____

_____

What can you do to build good working relationships with all of your co-workers?

_____

_____

Do you explain what the incentives and rewards are to each of the co-workers to inspire them toward excellence? If not, why not?

_____

_____

How do you handle the occasional outburst?

_____

_____

Reflections

Unmatched Priorities

What happens when you need a co-worker's help and she has completely different priorities and tasks? Take the following steps:

1. Find out what other projects are taking the co-worker's time.

2. If you know for a fact that these projects can't be put aside, ask your boss if there is someone else who can help.

3. If you are uncertain of the co-worker's priorities, both of you go to your boss and request suggestions. Then it is up to your boss to decide whether to put your co-worker's projects on hold or to assign someone else to the project.

If your co-worker has a different boss, arrange a short meeting to sort things out. You eliminate a lot of running trying to convey messages and assignments back and forth amongst yourselves. You all know where you stand in relation to the project.

Conflict Resolution

We all have different priorities, interests and work styles. Because of these differences, a certain amount of conflict is normal. It is not normal to allow a conflict to get so out of control that it jeopardizes the work that needs to be done.

Determining the real issue

Before you can resolve a conflict, you have to determine the issue. You must:

- **Remain objective.** Getting angry, hurt or taking the situation personally will make it difficult for you to evaluate and resolve the conflict.

- **Study the behavior patterns.** Understanding how the individual with whom you are in conflict is acting and collecting information about the reasons for this behavior will take you a long way toward resolution. Does this person have similar problems with others? Is this typical or unusual behavior? Is the person under considerable personal or professional stress?

- **Define what the stated problem is.** Do you see it as a point of conflict? If not, why? If so, what are the key points of contention? Write them down and try to deal with each one.

- **Other perspectives.** Get other perspectives and assessments of the conflict. Sometimes you are too close to the issue to objectively look at all aspects yourself.

Gathering information may instantly clarify the issue and lead to some solutions. Regardless of whether or not this happens, the next step is to communicate with whom you are in conflict and negotiate a solution. Otherwise you will both be wasting time that could be used for more positive activities.

Communication: The Key to Conflict Resolution

When you are communicating with someone who is angry or hostile, it is essential to remember these points:

- Clarify in your own mind what your objectives are in terms of resolving the conflict. These should include:

  — An approach to discussion that avoids confrontation

  — A solution that is fair to both parties

  — An outcome where hostility has been eliminated

  — A situation where clear communication has been established

- Don't be drawn into an argument, especially when it involves discussion of nonessential points or issues that are difficult to objectively measure. All the argument will do is waste time and obscure the issues as it descends into a subjective and nonproductive free- for-all.

- If you find that someone is trying to engage you in an argument, take the following steps to defuse it:

    — Listen to what is being said, but don't argue specifics.

    — Respond in terms of a larger nonarguable issue. (Shift the discussion toward a solution or to what is best for the company.)

- Avoid getting into these arguments by defining your purpose clearly and simply at the beginning of the conversation.

    — State that you know a problem exists and that you want it to be resolved for everyone's benefit.

    — Describe, impartially and objectively, your perception of the problem.

- Encourage the person to describe the problem and the frustrations that have caused it. Ask if the person agrees with your assessment of the problem and, if not, ask, "What do you think the problem is?"

- Listen to what the other person says without interruption, even if you disagree. Let these negative feelings be vented. More will be gained in terms of a long-term solution if these feelings are aired and not allowed to fester.

- Summarize objectively what you have heard. Even if you are angry or irritated, don't fall into the trap of responding to specific points or defending yourself. Instead, assure the other person that you have heard all that was said and that you understand. Getting angry or irritated will only raise the other person's defenses and that will make what you have said go unheard. ("Based on what you've told me, I understand why you feel …")

- If you find objective reasons for disagreeing, explain them. ("I understand your point about … but I think it's important to look at it from this angle …")

- Suggest solutions. Engage the individual in a discussion of the options. ("Here are some ideas I have for solving the problem. I'd like to know your reactions and your ideas. I think we can resolve this issue.")

- If the issues you are discussing are not the actual source of the conflict, cut through them until you reach the real issue and focus the discussion on that point.

- If you reach an impasse, call in a neutral third party to mediate the solution.

Remember, conflict takes two people. If, first, you don't allow yourself to be drawn into the conflict and, second, make the effort to solve it, you will save considerable time and energy. But most importantly, you will maintain control of yourself and the situation.

Handling Conflicts in the Office

It has come to your attention that one of your co-workers has a problem with you. She has announced it to a number of people and is making it difficult for you to complete your assignments on time because she is quickly raising barriers between you and the rest of your co-workers. The problem seems deep-seated and you are not exactly certain what triggered it. What steps do you take to resolve the conflict before it wastes more time and creates irrevocable barriers to working together?

1. What do you do to define and clarify the problem? Are you certain that you understand the underlying issues?

   _____

   _____

   _____

2. What do you do when someone is trying to engage you in an argument?

   _____

   _____

   _____

3. What can you say to defuse a volatile situation? How can you summarize what you are feeling?

   _____

   _____

   _____

Reflections

5 THE OFFICE: CONTROLLING YOUR TIME

Do you have a hard time saying "no" to a request from a colleague or a staff member? Even if it will completely upset your schedule or make it impossible for you to meet your own deadlines? If so, take heart. You are not alone. Many people find it difficult to refuse the requests of others. The reasons for this are varied and understandable:

- Telling someone "no" can be interpreted as rejection.

- Saying "no" can appear confrontational.

- You want to be liked and fear you will be disliked if you refuse someone's request.

- Being asked to do many things makes you feel important.

- You believe that being very busy and working hard will help your career.

You have to evaluate a request in terms of your own agenda. If your agenda isn't clear, you have to:

1. Review your priorities and assignments to see if this request fits within their boundaries.

2. Determine whether you are the best choice for this request or whether you are being asked because you never say "no."

3. Don't postpone your decision. Say "no" at once, but do take the time to explain why.

4. Suggest other possible solutions or alternative means that can be used to accomplish the task.

5. If you are in a position to make a contribution to the task but it is inappropriate for you to assume total responsibility, offer to answer questions, review materials, etc. Suggest specific times when you can help.

6. Understand that saying "no" does not have to mean rejection, to mean a confrontation or to result in bad feelings if handled in a friendly, matter-of-fact fashion.

7. Understand that saying "yes" all the time does not guarantee popularity or career advancement.

Delegate!

You can greatly increase the amount of time you have available each day and become more productive learning how to delegate effectively and appropriately. Delegating is assigning to others specific tasks and giving them the requisite authority to complete those tasks with mutually agreed-upon methods for evaluating the completed work. Simply put, it is giving someone a job and allowing them to do it within your guidelines.

Barriers to Delegating

You may find it difficult to delegate to others for a number of reasons. You may have had problems in the past when you assigned something and were disappointed in the results. You are a perfectionist and think that someone else can't do the job as well as you can. You are afraid that someone else will do the job better than you. You have no desire to take the time to provide adequate information or instruction for someone else to successfully complete the task.

These are all good excuses, but that is all that they are — excuses. When you delegate a job, you experience feelings attached to the transfer: loss of power, loss of authority, loss of achievement, loss of prestige and many other types of losses. Even though these are uncomfortable emotions that you would rather not have, the risk of delegating is worth it when you consider the benefits involved to your company and yourself. Take the chance and delegate. You will find that there are hidden talents in people once they are used to the idea of opening up and sharing their thoughts and feelings with the company instead of internalizing. Examine the barriers that you feel when it comes time for you to delegate. Analyze them for their validity and determine what you can do to lessen these feelings. Doing this examination will help you cope with your sense of loss as well as raise your "delegating consciousness."

Authority vs. Responsibility

Giving up authority is perhaps the most difficult aspect of delegating for many managers. If you want your employee to succeed, it is vital for you to give him the power to act, which means giving up a bit of your control. Without doing this, you cripple the employee's ability to initiate or even complete the project before he even has a chance to begin! It is also important that you inform all "players" connected to the project that you have given this authority to the employee.

However, giving authority does not mean giving up the responsibility for the task. The responsibility remains with you. You are the person who must make certain that the final product is completed. Establish checkpoints and other monitoring devices to make certain that the project is on the right target. Then you can relax and work on other tasks.

Effective Delegating

- Determine who is the most capable person for the task. Who has enough skill to perform the assignment in the time frame that you have available.

- Anticipate problems. If a person is inexperienced or fearful, make certain that there is adequate support available from others.

- Explain the assignment thoroughly. Hold a meeting or delegating conference where, in writing, you describe the task, including deadlines, monitoring plans, expectations, budgets and anything else important to the project. Go over these points with the person and make mutual changes to the plan to accommodate both of you.

- Communicate the results you want, not the methods used to achieve these results.

- Make certain that the person being assigned the task summarizes for you what is expected to confirm a basic understanding of the assignment.

- Make certain that you budget additional time for extra training. In the long run, taking time at the start of the delegating will provide you with an investment. Once your worker knows what you expect from a delegated task, future delegations will move much faster.

- Be realistic and fair in your demands and expectations so that everyone gains from the experience.

Delegate It

Review the rules for delegating and decide whether the following situations were handled properly.

1. Jean asked Carol to file a large set of papers away "whenever she could spare the time."

   _____

2. David and Bill took a longer lunch hour to go over a report that was due by both of them next week to make sure figures were accurate.

   _____

3. Harry sat down and had a meeting with Linda, Tom and Mike to discuss their roles in the upcoming end-of-month inventories.

   _____

4. John handed a report to his secretary, muttered something incoherent about needing it back this afternoon and walked out quickly.

   _____

5. Richard was asked to handle the installation of the new computer equipment in the office. When his boss found out that Richard knew almost nothing about computers, he sent someone else in to assist Richard with the task.

   _____

6. Thomas held a meeting with his staff for almost three hours, designating assignments left and right, and barking out deadlines. The staff people left the meeting feeling afraid, worried and upset.

   _____

7. Larry and Steve were involved in a high-priority project. Karen came over to Steve's desk asking for his help with some accounting problems. Steve understood Karen's plight and sent her to go see Grace, who was head of the accounting department.

   _____

Distractions

As we discussed in a previous chapter, there are many distractions in the office that sap your time. They all have one common characteristic: they divert you from the task at hand.

Techniques to avoid becoming distracted:

- Understand the real issues. You allow yourself to avoid completing a task by giving in to distractions. You need to ask yourself why.

- Ask if your distractions fit within your priority framework.

- Do you enjoy the diversions the distractions provide? Are they a problem regardless of whether you enjoy the task?

- When you feel yourself tempted by a distraction, stop and remind yourself of what your priorities are and what you stand to lose if you give in to the distraction.

- Don't be misled by the apparent urgency of the distraction. The squeaky wheel demands the most attention, but isn't necessarily of the highest priority.

- If you do think that the distraction warrants a higher priority than what you are working on, don't hesitate to clarify your priorities with your supervisor.

Don't give in to distractions unless you absolutely have to. You will be able to get so much more completed and increase your own sense of satisfaction of finishing a job on time and without stress.

Never Enough Time

Somehow you find yourself walking into the office each day determined to complete a project. You are eager to begin, but when the day ends, you depart feeling frustrated because you never had any time to work on it.

If this happens to you often, then it is time to do something about it. You have to take a serious and objective look at the reasons that you are not getting the work done in the time that you have. We will review some of the typical reasons why you can't get things done.

You feel overwhelmed

Either the project is so big that you have a hard time figuring out what you're going to do to get it done or you have too many things slated for the same time period.

If the project is too big, break it down into smaller, more manageable components. For instance, you must write an annual report for the entire company. Just the idea seems daunting. But if you break it down into chapters based on each division or section, such as Budget, Sales, Accounting, Marketing and such, you can concentrate on one section at a time. As you complete each section, you come that much closer to completing the entire task. It doesn't seem quite so large when you break it into smaller elements.

If the reason you are not getting something done is because of too much work and not enough time, see what projects you can delay until a later time or see whether you can delegate it to someone else. You have to complete the annual report, turn in statistics about the projected sales and evaluate all the employees in your section by the middle of next week. That leaves you five work days to get all this done. Look at the projects, decide what you must do yourself (such as the employee evaluations) and what you can give to another employee. The annual report is in various stages of completion and you alone know how you are working on it, so you can't delegate this, but the statistics are just gathered and not in any order. You write out what your expectations are and when the project is due. You call in an employee and spend 15 minutes reviewing the project. You give him all the information and all of the data.

Then you arrange for him to come back at the end of a week to review his progress. The task is now out of your hands, leaving you free to split your time between the evaluations and the annual report. Things seem less overwhelming when you call upon the resources and talents available to you in your staff.

You let yourself be distracted

As we said before, distractions can be a major deterrent to using your time well. They can be external (people dropping in or calling) or internal (daydreaming or not focusing your full attention on the project at hand.) If you feel like you aren't getting things done because of distractions, identify what it is that is distracting you and then find a way to alleviate it.

You don't get started because you don't have the time to finish

This excuse is reminiscent of feeling overwhelmed. You haven't looked at the entire project and decided how it should be done. If it is a huge project that will need large blocks of time devoted to its completion, decide how you can break it down into smaller parts. Then you won't have to devote all of your time and energy to the entire project, just specific tasks that can be completed in the time that you have available. Don't look at the big picture until you have all the smaller parts of it finished. Control your time, don't let it control you!

On Monday, Amanda was given a large and complex report to complete by Friday. She was overwhelmed by the size of the task and found herself trying to avoid starting it for almost the entire day on Monday. She tried to complete all of her other work before beginning the project, including tasks that she had been putting off for weeks. Why was she so reluctant to begin?

She felt overwhelmed by the size of the project. What steps could she take to make it easier?

_____

_____

_____

How should she set her priorities?

_____

_____

_____

What can she do to ensure that her focus is on the task at hand and not lost in a daydream?

_____

_____

_____

What do you do to handle your own distractions?

_____

_____

_____

Reflections

6 THE OFFICE: CRISIS TIME MANAGEMENT

Waiting until the last minute to start a project ends in panic because it doesn't allow enough time to complete it. Save yourself time and unnecessary worry with the following tips and techniques.

Deadline Crisis

You have a deadline for a project and you just don't think you are going to finish on time. As soon as you realize this, acknowledge it at once. The sooner you admit you are not going to meet a deadline, the more options you will have available to manage what could be a potential crisis. Don't commit professional suicide by waiting until the last minute to acknowledge that the work isn't going to be completed on time, regardless of whether you are directly responsible for its production or you've delegated it to a colleague.

Determine the best course of action and take it. Assign blame and other punishments later. At the moment, you have to determine how best to get the project done. Ask yourself: "Can I buy more time to complete this project? What are the ramifications of extending the deadline?"

- Examine all of the potential repercussions of delaying the project. How will the company suffer? The client? The co-workers? You?

- Then determine who decides whether the deadline can be extended. What is on their agenda that will be affected by the delay?

- Do you have a legitimate reason for not having completed this project and wanting this deadline extended?

Then, after you have asked these questions:

- Analyze the repercussions carefully. You must understand what problems will arise by changing a deadline. If you know them well, then you can counter objections and still enlist aid in getting the job done.

- Try to consider whether there are any opportunities that might be created by delaying the work. Will prices be affected? Will the delay cause a reassessment of the project's importance? Will the client lose business?

What will changing the deadline do to the person in charge of the impending deadline? Will this person lose stature? Be embarrassed? Suffer politically? Will the person receive any benefits from the delay?

Examining these issues will improve your chances of getting your deadline extended.

If It's Your Fault, Admit It

Do you have a legitimate reason for not completing this project on time? Don't rationalize or make excuses. If the answer is "no," you really need to acknowledge it to yourself and then later to others. If you need an extension, you will be able to negotiate more effectively if you don't make excuses. Just inform the boss that you will be able to get the assignment done once the deadline has been extended. This may or may not work, but at least you will be on record that you are willing to rectify any error in judgment you made regarding the deadline.

If others are responsible for creating the delay, avoid turning the situation into a confrontation. You will probably still need their cooperation to complete your project. You need to put blame and animosity aside and work together to get the task done in the new time frame allotted. You can't afford to create a conflict at this time. You have to get the job done. When it's done, then worry about the blame.

Don't spend time pointing fingers at others. Explain the situation in an organized, objective fashion, explaining the sequence of events and the responsibilities of various individuals without dwelling on their shortcomings.

Negotiating the New Deadline

If you have decided that a new deadline is cost-effective and will not have a detrimental impact on your company, then you need to negotiate a new deadline. Discuss it with whomever is authorized to extend the deadline. Keep it short and to the point; you are imposing on another person's time.

- Outline the situation.

- Acknowledge responsibility without blame or beating yourself up.

- Identify the repercussions (if any).

- Identify the opportunities that may arise by the delay (if any).

- Describe how you propose to solve the problem.

- Describe what additional resources you will need to complete the task.

- Summarize the situation, your solution and what your timetable is.

If you are responsible for the delay, be prepared to explain, but also move on to how you intend to solve the problem. Don't dwell on it.

Five Steps to Completing Any Task

Even if you can extend the deadline or find that you might still have time to finish the project without having to get extra time, you still have to get the project done. The following steps are useful even when you are not in crisis mode, but especially helpful when you are working against time rather than with it.

Step 1: Get focused

Clear your mind of all distractions, worries and anxieties about the deadline and any other mental flotsam you have floating around in your mind. You will never work productively if your mind is being pulled in six or seven directions. Take three deep breaths and focus on getting this task done one step at a time.

Step 2: Cut through the clutter

Anything on your desk that does not relate to your project is to be considered a distraction. Clutter represents unmade decisions and uncompleted business. However, when you are facing a deadline, it is not the time to suddenly decide to organize all the papers on your desk. Instead, move them off and have only the task at hand available. It will help you focus. Whatever you do, don't allow any additional mail or projects to be put on your desk until you have completed the task. Then you can go back and establish an organizational system based on the principles we discussed earlier in this book that will help you keep the clutter under control.

Step 3: Understand your priorities

You have a very limited time to complete the project. This is your top priority, especially if a deadline hangs over you. If two are conflicting, you need to decide at once how you are going to divide your time or delegate the second project so that both tasks will be completed. If you haven't done so by now, identify additional resources and recruit them immediately. To hesitate is to lose the momentum that you have gathered during the first two steps. Keep in mind the deadlines and plan accordingly.

Step 4: Avoid interruption

Allowing your highest priority to be interrupted is a form of avoidance. Don't allow it to happen.

- Have your calls held or unplug your phone.

- Don't allow any visitors that don't relate to the project at hand.

- Dedicate all available time on your calendar to the completion of the project. This means canceling or rescheduling nonessential meetings, appointments or lunches.

- If you have to come in early to get some quiet time to work on the project, don't allow the other early workers to distract you over donuts and coffee. You are coming in to work on your project, not to indulge in other activities.

Step 5: Do it

Budget at least one or two hours of uninterrupted time to organize what you need to do and another two hours to start working.

You have just taken over a project that you delegated to a subordinate. It is a mess. You have two days to complete it. Some of the information is useable, but you still have to decide what to use and what to discard. You know that you are responsible for the project's completion, but you don't think that in its present condition it will be done on time.

What steps do you have to take to make certain that:

1. You get more time to complete the project:

   _____

   _____

   _____

2. You get the focus that you need:

   _____

   _____

   _____

3. You cut the clutter to focus on the job:

   _____

   _____

   _____

4. You set the priorities:

   _____

   _____

   _____

5. You avoid interruptions:

   _____

   _____

   _____

Reflections

Getting Started

Often when you are under pressure to meet a deadline and the project is not even begun, you get this feeling of overwhelming anxiety. The task looks too hard and the time is too short.

The best remedy to all of this anxiety is to just get started.

Organize the project by drawing a circle on a piece of paper. Put the name of the project in the circle. Then start thinking of the things that you need to do to get the project done. Draw lines from the main circle, draw a small circle at the end of each line and label each circle with an item that needs to be done. Use the spokes of the wheel to represent ideas or points you want to make. The objective is to get as many ideas or components down on paper as possible. This will make it easier to organize all your ideas into an outline, which you can then follow to get the project done.

If you are supervising a project:

- Summarize your responsibilities.

- Outline the responsibilities and deadlines of other individuals involved.

- Establish checkpoints when various aspects of the project need to be monitored. Check the progress regularly. Make certain that you are working on time.

- When you have organized all that needs to be done, call a meeting, make assignments, answer questions, explain the deadlines and especially the checkpoints to monitor progress.

- Communicate responsibilities orally and in writing.

If you alone are responsible for the task:

- Set aside a minimum of two hours and begin work.

- Find a place where you will not be interrupted, even if you have to hide in a library.

- Identify whether you need to make arrangements for additional resources and support.

- Use the circle chart idea to break the project into manageable pieces.

- Establish your own checkpoints to monitor your progress. Know when each part is due and make certain that you are on time.

- If you have mental gridlock, tackle the one aspect of the task that you are most comfortable with — even if it is not the first step. This will open your mind to the rest of the project.

- Don't allow yourself to become distracted. Before you begin, get the coffee, sharpen the pencils, unplug the phone, straighten the pictures and all the other little time-fiddling distractions that you use to avoid the work. Let nothing distract you — even if you think that you will spend these initial two hours staring at a blank piece of paper. You won't. You will start working and once you start, it's coasting all the way.

Avoid Future Crises

Congratulations! You have managed to survive the deadline crisis. Now it's important for you to analyze how it came to be a crisis in the first place. You need to prevent this from happening again. Too many of these and your supervisors will begin to doubt your abilities to complete a project on time, and the stress will negatively affect you as well. You don't have to move from crisis mode to crisis mode. Instead, using the lessons that you learned from your latest crisis to help you manage your time well will alleviate the tension.

Ask yourself these questions. (And do yourself a favor: write down the answers and review them when you are next facing a deadline dilemma.)

- What did I do (or not do) to create this crisis?

- How did I allow myself to be distracted?

- How did I waste time?

- Are there unresolved problems that will create future crises? How do I resolve them?

- What role did conflict with others play in the situation?

- What did I learn from this situation?

- What steps can I take to prevent this situation from happening again?

No one really likes the pressure of a crisis situation (although many people actually think that they work better when the pressure is on). But everyone, at one time or another, finds themselves in this situation. The key is to look for ways to get out of the crisis with minimal stress, completing the assigned task. Then you need to take steps to avoid making the same mistake in the future.

Crisis Management

1. Have you ever been in a crisis, fighting against a deadline? Explain.

   _____

   _____

   _____

2. What did you do to complete the crisis project?

   _____

   _____

   _____

3. Did you effectively use your time? How?

   _____

   _____

   _____

4. Have you given someone a deadline before, and the task was not completed? Why not? How could you have helped? What could you have done differently?

   _____

   _____

   _____

5. What steps do you need to take to avoid future crises?

   _____

   _____

   _____

Reflections

7 HOME: TIME PLANNING FOR WORKING PARENTS

Working parents often feel guilty about being away from their families and strive to compensate by not "managing" as they would at work.

Setting Priorities at Home

Time allocation and management are basically the same at home as they are at work. You still have issues of delegating, crisis management, saying "no" effectively, dealing with distractions and being in control, to name a few. But no matter how organized you are at work, you may find that all of your carefully learned skills seem to vanish once you are confronted with the tasks at home. Don't let this happen to you. Your family is counting on you.

Chaos and disorder can be avoided. Identify your priorities. As working parents, you must function as a team to establish the overall goals and priorities that guide your family. Ask yourself:

- What kind of relationship do I want to have with my spouse?

- What examples do I want to set for my children?

- What is important to our quality of life?

- What do we need to do to have the kind of life that reflects what we think is important?

Once you have answered these questions individually, compare them to each other. Discuss the similarities and the differences and try to reach a consensus about the overall goals that you want to achieve as a family. If you have children who are old enough to understand the purpose of these goals, you may want to include some of their insights. It may help ease them into their new roles of responsibility if they feel included in the process of setting the family priorities. Once you have the general goals established, you can then create a workable priority framework that will structure your home and help you achieve your goals. In order to set a framework, you need to follow these basic guidelines:

- Keep priorities simple.

- Know when to be flexible.

- Everyone pitches in and helps (to the extent they are able) with the household tasks. This means you, your spouse, your children — everyone!

After you have established your priority framework, handling routine and crisis situations will be easier because you have a tool that will assist you in making consistent, well-grounded and objective decisions. You may be wondering how these "family goals and priorities" translate into practicality. It's one thing to set goals and such for an office where there are quantifiable means of measuring the progress of a project. But how do you quantify what happens at home? Perhaps you don't, but you can set up systems that will enable you and your family to handle all the situations that occur each day.

Facing the Day

Do you find that chaos reigns supreme in the morning? Are you trying to do it all at one time? You know the drill: you and your spouse are trying to get ready for work, getting breakfast for the children, sending them off to school or taking them to day care, making lunches, washing dishes and so on. Let's face it, in most families, weekday mornings are not prime quality time.

Setting a morning routine cuts the chaos and makes the day a more pleasant experience for everyone. The hectic pace is under control and there is less of a tendency to forget important things.

Here are some ways to minimize the morning chaos and get the day going right:

- You and your spouse should get up about 30 minutes before the children. In fact, one of you should get up about 15 minutes before the other. This early rising will provide you with just enough of a head start to minimize the tension that happens when everyone is trying to get up and get organized all at once. As one of you is well into the morning routine, the other partner rises and begins his or her routine. Begin preparing breakfast, then wake the children and have them begin their morning procedures.

- Planning from the night before reduces morning stress.

  — Set aside 15 - 30 minutes each evening to sit down with the kids and organize the following day. Find out what's on their schedules and assign tasks for the next day. This alleviates barking orders in the morning and forgetting important appointments in the chaos of beginning the day.

  — Decide on breakfast for each day the night before and share responsibility for its preparation among family members old enough to fix it.

  — Make lunches the night before. Have the children, if they are old enough, help with this. You can set out the ingredients for the lunches and then let the kids help you assemble them.

  — Have everyone choose their clothes the night before. Make certain that the children are included in this process to avoid problems in the morning if they don't like what you have chosen.

— If there are special needs for the next day, make certain that you know what they are: money for a school outing, permission slips, baseball uniforms, homework assignments, whatever. Make sure that everything is organized and packed so that in the morning all you or your child has to do is grab the bag (or backpack) and the lunch and go.

— If your children are slow starters in the morning, wake them 15 - 20 minutes earlier and allow them to lounge around and enter the day slowly.

— Write out instructions for the baby-sitter/day-care center either the night before or during your quiet time before everyone else is up. Review it before you leave.

— Be flexible. Things happen and you have to learn to take them in stride. Have contingency plans in place on what to do if you have a sick child, sick baby-sitter, or if you get sick. Be prepared for snow days or school closures. In short, have systems in place so you can handle these situations efficiently. There is nothing worse than being confronted with a crisis situation at 6:30 a.m. There is no way you can handle it effectively without a backup plan.

As you can see, using your time effectively in the morning means that you need to allocate time the night before to take care of the routine chores that eat up time in the morning, when everyone is trying to leave at around the same time. By taking a half hour the evening before, you can eliminate much of the stress that accompanies doing too many tasks at one time. Adjust your schedule so that you can make the morning as pleasant as possible. It can set the tone for everyone's day.

- Establish house rules and make clear what is expected from family members.

  — Tell them the reasons. They will appreciate the honesty.

— Encourage them to suggest ideas for helping. Allow them to discuss the different jobs that need to be done and how they should be accomplished. This way they understand what they are getting into.

— Let them choose a task that they want to do. Make them realize that once the tasks have been assigned, they are responsible for completing them. This is nonnegotiable.

— Don't be drawn into an argument about why they have to do a particular chore.

- Above all, be consistent. Don't backslide. It will only send a message that you are not serious.

- Be flexible. This may seem like a contradiction, but in some instances it makes sense to bend the rules. If you do so, don't do it arbitrarily. Make certain that everyone understands why the rules have been changed.

The Point System

Set up a reward system based on points for chores. You can even determine allowances based on the points that are accumulated.

1. You and your spouse agree on the tasks that need to be done and then assign a point value for each task. For instance, 5-point tasks: cleaning the garage, sweeping the driveway, etc.; 3 points: setting the table, clearing the table. Base your points on how hard the task is and how long it takes. Make certain that you have comparable jobs that are dependent on your children's skills and ages.

2. Each person contracts to do a fixed number of points for each week, dependent on his or her ability and fixed time constraints.

3. Cut chips out of construction paper and write the job description on one side and the point value on the other. Make certain that you

have special chips for the "little ones" and that these are on different colored paper.

4. "Fish" for the jobs. Each family member chooses a chip, point side up, and then turns the chip over to find out what job was chosen. All members should keep drawing until the agreed number of points for each person has been reached.

5. Make a master list of tasks. Include the time of day when they are to be completed and post it where everyone can refer to it.

Evening Survival

One of the most stressful times of the day for many families is early evening. The parents come home from work tired and hungry, the kids are hungry and no one is in the mood for "quality time." How can you avoid turning this time of day, when you should be unwinding, into a nightmare? Don't just park your kids in front of the television to get some peace. Get control of this time and turn it into something pleasant.

Review your priorities. Do they include talking about one another's day? Sitting down together for dinner? Spending quality time with your kids? Once you have reviewed them, decide what you want to do and spend a little time doing it. Remember, you control the situation. Don't let it control you.

- Plan ahead for dinner if possible. Decide what can be done ahead of time and what can't.

- Assign responsibilities to your children (if they are old enough) like setting the table, getting out the dishes, helping you make the salad, feeding the dog, etc.

- Cook and freeze meals over the weekend, so that all you have to do when you or your spouse gets home is defrost and heat. This saves loads of time.

- Plan menus for the week and post them. Shop accordingly.

- Prepare your own "fast foods" ahead of time: biscuit mixes, pancakes, cut veggies and have them ready for use.

Beware of TV

Television is a convenient way to escape from doing your chores. This does not mean that only your children can be drawn into it, but you as well. Manage the time that the television is on. When there is work to be done, turn it off.

Evaluate the amount of time that you and your family watch TV. How does this fit within your family's goals and priorities? Determine if you have a better use for the time.

Make watching TV an active decision, not an automatic reaction. Don't just come into the room and turn on the set. Check the TV listings and choose the programs you are going to watch. When you are not watching the TV, turn it off. You will find that you have gained many hours to accomplish the things that you want to do. You will be able to get all the chores done and spend quality time with your family pursuing your goals.

1. Make a list of your family's goals. With them, prioritize and discuss ways of meeting them. Give them a time frame.

   a. _____

   b. _____

   c. _____

   d. _____

   e. _____

   f. _____

   g. _____

   h. _____

   i. _____

   j. _____

2. Make a menu for the week and estimate the time of preparation needed for each meal. What can you prepare ahead and freeze to use when you are seriously pressed for time?

3. Get double the mileage out of your cooking by doubling recipes and freezing them in microwaveable TV dinner trays.

4. How much TV do you and your family watch? Explore alternative entertainment ideas and enjoy them together. When was the last time you played a table game or worked on an arts and crafts project together?

Reflections

8 HOME: ORGANIZING

Just like your office, your home needs to be organized so that you can get things done. Whether you are single and live alone (or with a roommate) or have a family and home, unless things are organized, you will run out of time to get it all done. If you have papers strewn throughout the house and bills laying about, something is going to be forgotten. Don't let this happen to you.

If you've allowed your house (or apartment) to get out of control, don't plan on getting organized in one day or over the weekend. After all, it took longer than that to get to its current state, right?

The first thing you have to do is make a commitment to organize your house. Just as you divided large unmanageable tasks that seemed daunting and impossible to do at the office, you need to break down projects at home into smaller, more manageable pieces. Plan to do one room, a drawer or a closet at a time — whatever you can do without disrupting your entire life. Once you've organized an area, make sure that you and everyone else involved in your household agrees to maintain it that way.

This doesn't mean that you can never leave a cup on the dining room table again overnight, but it does mean making the effort to keep things neat and orderly in the future.

How on Earth Did This Mess Happen Anyway?

Good question. And one that you should answer before you set off to organize. How did you allow the place to get in this disorganized state in the first place? Think about how you manage each day and then determine what you can do to make every system (or nonsystem) work more effectively.

Do you pick up the house as you go along throughout the week or do you wait until the weekend and plan to do it all at once? If you normally are the type who does it all at once, consider doing a little each day. If the weekend suddenly turns hectic and you don't have time to pick up, you may find yourself waiting another week for the next weekend to pick up after two weeks' accumulation.

You don't have time to pick up during the week? Take 15 minutes at the beginning of the day or before you go to bed (get up a little early or stay up a little later) and pick up the day's things. Also pick up stuff when you have a few extra minutes during the day. You have clothes in the dryer or the stew is cooking? Do something else while you wait. Also, before you leave a room, look around and see what you can take with you and put away. It's a good way to use your time and save you effort down the line.

Time Enough

Sometimes, no matter how carefully you plan and organize, there just isn't enough time to get everything done. A wild, busy weekend may mean that the house suffers. It's okay. You don't have to devote every waking moment to taking care of things. But if you don't want to have twice as much work to do later, you may want to consider certain ways to help you get control.

- **Set deadlines.**

  You have deadlines at the office, you have deadlines at home. The reason that you never seem to get things done at home is that you left all the good structures that you created at the office. Once you get home, you adopt a "laissez-faire," "I'll get it done tomorrow" attitude. You are never going to get things done if this is how you think. Set yourself a specific deadline to get you going.

- **Do your least favorite jobs first.**

  Hate doing laundry? Despise cleaning the bathroom? Do these first. It gets them over with and alleviates the feeling of dread that you are going to have to do them once you are done with all the other work. You won't spend the entire time you are doing your tasks thinking of ways to avoid the ones you can't stand. Getting them done also makes the rest of your chores go faster because you aren't finding reasons to avoid the dreaded laundry or bathroom.

- **Schedule major projects in advance.**

  Decide what major projects are and then establish a work schedule to get them done. Then stick to the plan. If you want to paint the house, decide what steps need to be taken: choose the colors, buy the paint and supplies, decide the weekend that you will begin by preparing and priming (with a rain-date scheduled as well if you are working outdoors) and decide the weekend(s) that you will need to complete the exterior painting. Then plan the amount of time that each task needs and block off that time accordingly. (Always start at the back of the house, since this is the place least likely to be seen. If the front is completed first, you may find yourself putting it off again and again.)

- **Maintain a master calendar.**

  This is an important communications tool that will keep you and your family current about what plans are being made and what events are occurring. It will show you when your deadlines are and where conflict may occur, allowing you to reschedule.

- **Don't bite off more than you can chew.**

  If you say you are going to paint the house in one weekend or re-tile the basement, you may get the jobs done, but the experience might change your mind. Break the big jobs down into manageable parts.

- **Use lists.**

  One of the simplest and most effective ways to ensure that you get everything done is to make a list. Make daily, weekly and monthly lists indicating things that need to be accomplished within those time frames. Also make sure that you include errands and small jobs that you can work on as you go along.

Make a list of everything you need to get done in the next month. Circle the tasks you feel are the most important.

_____

_____

_____

_____

_____

_____

_____

_____

_____

_____

_____

_____

_____

Go back to the tasks you have circled. Do they outnumber the smaller, less important tasks? Give your reasons why or why not.

_____

_____

_____

Reflections

Paperwork? At Home?

That's right, you have to do paperwork at home as well as at the office. It makes it so much easier if your papers are kept in some kind of order for easy reference. Think about it. At home you have everything from recipes to insurance policies, warranties to coupons. Are you going to keep all these things jumbled in a couple of drawers? Not if you want to find them quickly, you won't.

If you don't have a home filing system for your important papers, create one now. Gather all of your important papers and then organize them. Put your warranties in one file, important health and insurance documents in another, coupons in a third and so forth. Clearly mark them and place them in some kind of home filing system — a desk, a strongbox, a small file cabinet — where you can easily get to them. Add appropriate folders as you go along.

Mail

It's easy to just skim through the mail, see what interests you and put the rest aside for later. But if you are honest, you will admit that the mail pile just keeps growing and growing.

When you get mail at home, use the same TAF (toss, act on it, file) system that you use at the office. Open each piece and decide what to do with it. You can toss it in the trash, add it to the "to pay" folder, add it to the "to do" file or permanently file it. Few things come in your mail that you want to hold onto and refer to later.

You gotta have a system

Develop a system. It doesn't have to be complex or elaborate. It just has to be easy to follow. The best systems are the simplest because you are more apt to follow them.

Keep a special pad of paper on the counter and ask family members to jot down grocery items you need to pick up at the store. Establish one place, maybe on the refrigerator where family members can check for phone messages. Keep the master calendar outlining the entire family's activities in a central area of the house.

Don't be a "pack rat"

Don't allow yourself to clutter your home with unused items. Too often we buy things or hold on to things with the thought "One day this may come in handy." If you are a pack rat or a potential pack rat, here are some guidelines to help you reform.

- **Have a place for everything and put everything in its place.**

  It takes longer to tidy up a house than it does to clean it. The more things that you have, the harder it is to get everything put away. How often have you heard people talk about cleaning their houses before the housekeeper comes? What they mean is that they have to pick up the clutter before the housekeeper can clean.

  Everything — keys, groceries, dirty clothes, cat food — should have its own place in your house. If they don't, assign one and make certain that everyone knows where it is. This not only helps you to keep clutter-free but avoids you having to sarcastically reply "hanging on my ear" when your child demands "Mom, where is my …?"

- **Be practical.**

  How many pairs of jeans do you have in your closet that you are saving until you lose 10 more pounds. How long have you had them? If it's been a year or more and your closet is bulging, get rid of them. You are looking for an excuse to keep them when you really don't need them.

  The same thing goes for equipment and games. Do you have a basketball in the garage that looks older than you? Is it flat? Are you ever going to fill it and play? If your answer is no, get rid of it. If the answer is yes, do it now and start playing, or you, too, are just making excuses.

- **Inspired to do more? Then do it!**

  If you are cleaning your closet or the garage and it seems easier than usual, keep going. Don't stop, but get rid of as much stuff as you can. You never know when the mood will strike you again.

- **Handle paper as you come to it.**

  Read the mail as it comes in. Do what you have to do with it, read it, toss it or put it in the "to pay" folder. Even if you don't mail the bill at once, write the check and put it with the bill on the "to mail" pile with the date that you are going to send it out. Then all you have to do is review it and send it to the payee.

  When it comes to the newspaper, another item that has the tendency to pile up into huge daunting stacks, either read it when you get it or set a time limit as to how long you will keep it. Check with your city regarding recycling of papers. You may have to store them and then take them to a recycling area at a scheduled time.

- **Avoid impulse buying.**

  To save time and money, go to the store with a specific list of what you need and stick to it. (Grocery stores cleverly place small items, such as razors, gum, candy, magazines, cookbooks, etc., at the checkout counter to encourage impulse buying when people are relaxing and waiting to pay for their goods. The customers are not really thinking about what they are purchasing or how much more they are spending when they toss these additional "little things" into their shopping carts.) How many magazines that looked good at the store come into your house and are never looked at again?

  The same goes for buying other things. A woman would go to a craft store once a month and purchase "just a little something." It didn't have to be very big — a kit, a ceramic cup, a potter's wheel, silk flowers — but these items began to accumulate until she had an entire room filled with half-completed projects and useless, dust-catching "objets d'art." It took almost three consecutive weekends for the woman's family to help her clear out the room when they found that they needed it.

With a little work and planning, you can organize your home into a clutter-free environment.

The Clutter Quiz

Take this little clutter test to help you identify your areas of strength and weakness. It will help you control your surroundings.

Please rate these questions from 1 (doesn't bother me) to 5 (help me, I am drowning in clutter). And please answer these honestly. There is no score, but you can see where you are and how far you have to go.

1. My house seems to double its clutter on a daily basis. I just keep tripping over more stuff.

2. I am tired of being buried in an avalanche of stuff whenever I open any closet door in this house.

3. I need more space that I can really use. Too much of it is wasted and what I do have I don't know what to do with.

4. I have tried bribing my kids to get them to help.

5. My spouse and my kids have trouble finding anything in their rooms.

6. I need to have an organized, user-friendly kitchen. I feel like we are all jogging 5 miles a day trying to get dinner on the table.

7. I hate cleaning. I hate laundry. I hate chores. I must find a way to streamline and delegate some of these responsibilities.

When you have finished this quiz, make a list of the areas in your home that need your special attention: closets, drawers, living room, bathroom, etc. Now answer these questions:

What is my favorite job around the house?

_____

What is my least favorite job?

_____

Now get started!

Reflections

9 STAND BY FOR MIND CONTROL

Just as you have organized your office and your home, you need to take the time to organize yourself. If you don't have your mind and feelings under control, you are apt to become overwhelmed and ineffective.

One of the biggest time-wasters you can experience is stress. When you are under stress, you are unable to focus on the tasks at hand and are easily distracted. You also are often depressed and have a low level of energy. Add these together and you find that it adds up to much wasted time and resources.

Overwhelmed?

Are you worried, guilty, depressed, anxious or feeling other negative emotions? These are often the results of internal conflict. There are many situations that can trigger these feelings, but they are usually produced when you experience disappointment or when you have unresolved fundamental issues. Some of the most typical of these triggers are:

- Worrying about meeting the expectations of others.

- Feeling inadequate (through a lack of achievement in your professional or personal life).

- Feeling anxious about how others perceive you.

- Feeling guilty about time wasted and opportunities missed.

- Feeling guilty about lack of involvement with family and friends.

- Unresolved conflicts with co-workers, bosses, your spouse, your family, your children or anyone else who is or has been important to you.

Stress can cause these conflicting emotions and render you virtually ineffective. Everyone experiences stressful situations and emotions at one time or another. This is as inevitable as death and paying taxes. However, allowing these things to overwhelm you and essentially put your life on hold — at work or at home — is in your control.

Stress and Conflict: What Are the Real Issues?

Too often we take out our anger, disappointment and frustration on the wrong persons or for the wrong reasons. If your spouse, your child or your colleague does something to upset you and you overreact, there is a chance you are not reacting to what actually happened but to an unresolved issue you have buried.

To avoid doing this and upsetting not only yourself but the other person so that no one is acting efficiently or wisely, you need to ask yourself a series of questions. Be brutally honest with yourself; no one else will. You must identify what is really driving your feelings. It is a hard task, but in order to be able to control your reactions and your stress levels, you have to step back and look at why you are behaving and reacting the way that you are. Getting some perspective on how you react to various situations is a way to conduct a self-assessing dialogue with yourself. Understanding the problem is half the solution. Understanding yourself and how you behave gives you the impetus for change.

When you find that you are overreacting to a situation, step back and ask:

- How was I feeling before I became angry?

- Is there a pattern to these negative feelings?

- Are they triggered by certain types of situations (e.g., intimacy,

having to make professional or personal commitments, being
evaluated by others)?

- How do I feel when I am corrected or criticized by someone? Do I
  tend to respond in a predictable way?

- Am I frequently disappointed by others? In what types of situations
  (work or family)?

Changing Your Behavior

When you are not experiencing internal conflict, it is relatively easy to deal
with problems created by others. While you may be upset and angry, there is
still a level of detachment that allows you to maintain a certain objectivity.

When you are experiencing internal conflict, you need an outlet for pent-
up, negative feelings. You feel very intense, emotional and subjective. You
won't be able to resolve these issues by dumping your bad feelings on others.
It might make you feel better temporarily, but you haven't done anything to
prevent the situation from occurring again. You have wasted time and energy,
and most importantly, you haven't resolved or improved the way you feel on a
fundamental level.

When you find yourself overreacting:

- Take an honest reading of your feelings.

- Try to step outside yourself and observe the dynamics of the
  situation in a detached manner.

- Identify the real source of your anger or frustration. What are you
  experiencing? Can you identify it as extreme disappointment, a loss
  of control, feeling inadequate, feeling unappreciated?

- Verbalize your feelings in a nonconfrontational way, if possible.
  Describe why you feel angry, frustrated, inadequate, etc. If it is not
  appropriate to express these feelings at the time, create
  opportunities as soon as possible.

While these mental exercises may help, don't reject the possibility of discussing some of these issues with a counselor, minister, psychologist or close friend.

The objective is to remove the chronic causes of stress and conflict in your life so you can accomplish more and enjoy your work, family and friends.

Think about a time you really lost your temper and overreacted. What was the cause of your outburst? Who was involved? What were you experiencing? How verbal did the dispute become? Was a resolution reached? Why or why not? What else could you have done to alleviate the situation? Were you responsible? Did you identify the real source of your anger? Did you verbalize your feelings in a nonconfrontational way? If the same situation were to repeat itself, what would you do differently?

_____

_____

_____

_____

_____

_____

_____

_____

_____

_____

_____

_____

_____

_____

_____

_____

_____

Reflections

Style

Everyone approaches work and tasks differently. It is important to understand your own personal style. How do you work best? What do you do to identify the barriers that prevent you from enjoying the level of productivity and fulfillment you desire?

What style do you prefer?

- Do you prefer to deal with the "big picture" and conceptualize or leave that to others and handle the detail work or the implementation?

- Do you typically "shoot from the hip" when making decisions or are you more methodical in considering all the data before taking a step?

- Do you prefer to work alone or as part of a team?

- Does everything have to be done perfectly?

- Are you comfortable supervising others?

Once you have determined what your style of work is, then you need to do the following:

- Determine what types of activities or approaches you are most comfortable with as well as those that make you uncomfortable.

- In those areas where you are uncomfortable, determine whether or not this discomfort is a barrier that is causing you stress and preventing you from getting things done.

If, for instance, you need to supervise others and you are uncomfortable doing so, it will be difficult for you to delegate effectively and manage a project that involves others. You may need to take steps to increase your comfort level with supervising. If you are really uncomfortable in supervising, you may need to ask for someone else to take over the supervision of the project.

Based on what you've determined your personal style is, you define how you work the most productively. Enhance that style, both at work or at home, by making an effort to remove any barriers that inhibit your ability to get things done.

Finally, don't worry about trying to imitate the styles of other people. Be yourself. It is the most comfortable, efficient and gratifying way to get things done.

Procrastination

Procrastination just postpones the inevitable. If what you are postponing is unpleasant, procrastinating just makes the task look even more undesirable. Remember, if you do the task you dread first, then the rest of the work is that much easier — whether in your personal or professional life.

If you procrastinate because you lack confidence in your abilities, avoiding the situation only enlarges these negative feelings and erodes your sense of self-esteem and self-worth. If the task is at home, for example, painting the house or wallpapering the bedroom, and you find yourself overwhelmed, step back and see what you can do to make yourself handle the task better. Putting it off will only increase your sense of failure. Then you will never get started.

The same goes for this type of procrastination at the office. Ask for assistance or training if you feel that you are inadequately prepared for the task at hand. If this option is not available, try to divide the task into manageable components and get started. Then assess what additional training you need after you complete your tasks. Additional training will increase your sense of adequacy.

When you find yourself procrastinating, give yourself these boosts to getting started:

- Ask yourself why you are procrastinating. Are you afraid you can't perform the task? Do you feel that it is inappropriate for you to do? Are you intimidated by the responsibility? Are you fearful of making errors?

- Review your priorities. Assess what the negative effect of avoiding the task will have on them. Also, really look at how it makes you feel and your sense of self-worth when you don't get a job started.

- Break the task into small parts and begin doing the one you dread the most.

- Set a deadline for completing a task and commit yourself to it by publicly telling others whom you can't afford to disappoint. For instance, you really are fearful of wallpapering your daughter's room, but you promised your daughter that it would be done for her slumber party in three weeks.

- Evaluate the reasons why you procrastinate and take steps to change your behavior.

The Perfectionism Trap

Are you a perfectionist?

Do you set unreasonable standards for yourself?

Do you feel guilty if you don't measure up?

Do you worry that people won't like you or won't approve of you if everything you do isn't perfect?

When you are complimented, do you feel that you don't deserve the praise?

Do you tend to procrastinate or dawdle when working on something that will be evaluated by others? Are you reluctant to hear feedback (positive or negative)?

If you answered "yes" to more than one of these questions, you are on your way or already are a perfectionist. As a perfectionist, you will find that you have a hard time getting things done. To avoid failure, you tend to put off completing a task. By dawdling you fail to get anything done, which can have even more serious repercussions than if you had completed the project imperfectly but satisfactorily in a timely manner.

There are certain things that you can do to get yourself out of the perfectionism trap. You have to commit yourself to the idea that getting the project done (at home or at work) by the designated deadline is your highest priority. You are responsible for these things, so stop wasting time and do them. Even if you make an error or it is not perfect, you need to get it done.

Make certain that you fully understand the expectations of those who will evaluate your work before you begin. Ask the important questions. What is the project to achieve? How polished does it need to be? How urgent is the project? What is the deadline? Write down the expectations and be very careful to ask about anything that confuses you or makes you doubt your ability to do a good job.

Learn that fine tuning, revising and continually tinkering with a project is just another way to avoid completing it. Do your best work and finish by the deadline.

Don't defeat yourself. Don't become so involved with the project that it becomes a part of you. Don't invest so much of yourself in the task that you fail to maintain a detachment. Make sure that you evaluate what you have done in direct relation to your list of expectations.

Establish a personal deadline for finishing a task that you take as seriously as the imposed deadline. This will give you a bit of extra time to polish the task to suit your perfectionist tendencies.

Get feedback when you have completed a task. If the reaction to the job you have done is reasonable and positive and the critique is constructive, it will enable you to look at the entire scope of the project and free you to be less than perfect.

Prime Time

For everyone, there is a time of day when we sparkle. For some, they work most efficiently in the morning. For others, it's after lunch and in the evenings. You need to identify your prime hours — when you work most efficiently and thus get the most accomplished.

Finding your prime time is simple. Observe how you handle detailed tasks and projects at various times of the day. If you seem to concentrate better in the morning, before lunch, then that's your prime time. Save your routines for after lunch when your creativity and focus is less keen.

Following your energy cycle will help you do the difficult tasks because you have the stamina and drive to do them. Organize your top priority projects and those that need intense concentration when you are at your "high" times.

Ideally, you should be able to conform your tasks to the time when you are at your best. While this is not always possible, you may be able to arrange your chores and assignments to come as close as you can to when your biological rhythms dictate are your high and low times.

Prime-time energy doesn't mean that you can't do other things during the rest of the day. It merely affords you a personal time that you can control when you are at your peak performance.

What's Your Style?

Take a good look at yourself. Examine your work habits and your activities. Do you procrastinate? Are you a perfectionist? What can you do differently?

1. What causes you the most stress?

   _____

   _____

2. When you finish a job, do you turn it in right away or do you continue tinkering with it?

   _____

   _____

3. What is your prime time of day? How do you use it?

   _____

   _____

4. What activities are you most comfortable doing?

   _____

   _____

5. What feelings trigger your own internal conflict? What can you do to avoid or stop them?

   _____

   _____

6. What steps do you take to make certain that you spend enough time with family and friends?

   _____

   _____

Reflections

10 TIPS, STRATEGIES AND TIMESAVING TECHNIQUES

Throughout this book, our goal was to help you organize your time so that you can do everything that you want to do. In this chapter we offer you not only the top 12 tips that will help you get things done, but another 38 ways to organize yourself into the calm, efficient person that you want to be.

1. **Use lists.** Keep track of all the things you need to get done by using lists. Writing down what you need to do and checking it off will help you visualize what needs to be done and how far along you are at completing your tasks.

2. **Maintain a time management organizational system calendar.** Record your appointments, activities, meetings, ideas, and personal and professional reminders. Be careful to transfer all pertinent information to your office calendar as well as on the one you maintain at home for your family.

3. **Set written goals and priorities.** Think about and record what it is you really want to accomplish, both short-term and long-term, personally and professionally, on paper. Keep copies at the office, at home and in your personal organizer. Refer to them often to stay on track. As you reach each goal or complete each task listed in your priorities, cross it off the list.

4. **Build strong working relationships with others.** Others will then be more likely to assist you when you need the help. Take the time to establish these relationships long before you think that you will need them. It will make your work life much easier and far more pleasant.

5. **Do the worst first.** Do what you hate the most before allowing yourself to work on what you like. Clean the bathroom before you arrange the flowers. By doing this, you not only get these things out of the way, but your other tasks go faster and are more enjoyable.

6. **Identify time-wasters and eliminate them.** There are many things that we have to deal with that rob us of valuable time. Identify these wasters and eliminate them.

7. **Take control of your time.** Don't let the amount of time you have control what you get done. You determine what needs to be done and allocate the right amount of time to do it.

8. **Organize your home and office.** Disorganization is one of the

biggest time-wasters there is. Follow the tips given in the book and later in this chapter to organize your home and office.

9. **Use the right equipment.** If you need a computer to effectively do your job, get one. Don't let outdated equipment rob you of valuable time. Think of ways to get them and then do it.

10. **Say "no."** Learn how to say "no." You can get snowed under and be working twice as hard as you should be unless you learn to say "no" politely. Only say "yes" when the request fits within your priorities.

11. **Delegate.** There is no rule that says you have to do it all. Learn how to delegate work — at the office and at home.

12. **Just do it.** Don't waste your time worrying about things that have no bearing on the job at hand. When you have a job to do, whether you are cleaning the car or writing a presidential speech, forget everything else and do the job.

13. **Be flexible.** Use your lists as guidelines, not iron law. If a hailstorm interrupts your plans for a picnic, have a secondary plan ready.

14. **Push yourself.** You will never know how much you can do unless you set your expectations high. When you feel overextended, weed out the activities of lowest priority. Constantly upgrade your accomplishments.

15. **Take care of the small stuff at once.** If it's only going to take a second, like signing a letter or winding a toy, do it. They will only come back again and again until you do, so get it over with and then tell the interrupter that you are not to be disturbed again.

16. **Don't procrastinate.** Once you start putting things off and find that it works once, you will have a tendency to do it again and again. Ease into your tasks and gather momentum.

17. **Don't try to be perfect.** Unless you are the catcher on the flying trapeze and working without a net, don't try to be perfect. Go for excellence instead.

18. **Separate the responsibilities of office and family.** Don't update your home lists at the office or bring a crammed briefcase home. If you work at home, designate a specific work space and keep regular hours there.

19. **It's okay to work extra hours sometimes, but don't make a habit of it.** This is a good indicator that you are not using time correctly. Reassess your agenda and don't take on more than you are capable of completing.

20. **Minimize interruptions.** Discourage visitors politely. When you are interrupted, stand or look as if you are busy and don't invite the visitor to sit down.

21. **Schedule meetings close to lunch or quitting time.** This simple way to schedule will keep the participants from pursuing irrelevant discussion. Start on time, use an agenda and summarize the accomplishments.

22. **Hire the best people.** When you have good people working for you, their competence will make your job easier and will reflect well on your judgment. You will also have the advantage of only having to train them once and then let them work independently under your authority.

23. **Discuss your ambitions with your boss.** Ask for reviews and discuss career ladders, raises and training. Volunteer for new responsibilities that fit within your career goals.

24. **Unclutter your desk.** Get rid of everything from the top of your desk but the project that you are working on. File away your papers.

25. **Create workable files.** Find a system that works for you and stick with it. You may use color folders, tabs, vertical files, whatever, but

just create some broad categories and make certain that you file your documents away as soon as you can.

26. **Take a break.** Take a few moments and clear your head. Stand up, take a walk, get a drink of water. Do something diverting. You will actually be gaining time by reviving your energy and spirit. Work will go much more smoothly.

27. **Make all phone calls at one time.** Put the phone where it is easy to reach and consider getting a shoulder rest so that your hands can be free to take notes.

28. **Create a directory.** Use a card file, a rolodex or the computer. The important thing is to have the numbers you use easily accessible. Don't waste time looking the numbers up in the phone book.

29. **Don't feel that you have to talk at an inconvenient time.** Make arrangements to call back later. Do this with friends, family, clients and co-workers. Unless it is an emergency, try to call back later. You may want to consider an answering machine if these calls are constant.

30. **Lay clothes out, make lunches and check schedules the night before.** Don't wait for the a.m. crunch time to decide what you want to wear, want to eat or have to do.

31. **Do two things "for the price of one."** When you are watching television, do some of the mindless tasks such as clipping coupons, mending or ironing. Keep a project box of small things that need to be done along with repair tools so that when you are watching TV or a video, your hands are busy.

32. **Take a folder of clippings with you at all times.** While waiting for meetings to begin, appointments to start or even at the doctor's office, have your reading folder with you and use this "dead time" to play catch-up with all the articles that you want to read but don't have time to do in the normal course of your day.

33. Convert routine tasks into "adventures" with your kids. Use errand time to spend some individual time with your children. Take them shopping and let them help. Point out interesting things and discuss what they want to talk about.

34. Keep a stockpile of special things for unexpected guests. This way when people drop in, you can whip something up to serve without fuss or bother. It saves a lot of time running to the store or ordering in.

35. Don't accumulate. Get rid of single-use appliances or things that you haven't used in over a year.

36. Foster independence in your children. The more self-reliant everyone in the family is, the better for you all. Assign chores early on and increase the responsibility as the children age.

37. If you can, hire help. Hire neighborhood teens to help at parties. They will appreciate the money and you won't have to do all the work. If someone offers to help, say "yes."

38. Don't grocery shop more than once a week. Settle on one store, take a list and stick to it. The best times to shop are before 11:30 a.m., in the evenings and on rainy days. Don't go during rush hour. Avoid Saturday shopping.

39. Cook ahead of time. Make a roast, stew or ham and serve variations during the week. Use the weekends to make freezer meals like spaghetti sauce, chili and other foods that can be frozen, then thaw them during the week for the family dinner. This also is a good way for single people to have nutritious meals and avoid the drive-through trap.

40. Pick up a mess as it's generated. The more you let it accumulate, the longer it will take to straighten up.

41. Keep it simple. Don't complicate your life. Don't impulse buy items that you won't use. Get rid of that clutter. Make schedules that are easily understandable and can be followed.

42. Know your energy cycle. If you are a morning person, plan your hardest and most challenging activities early in the day. If your energy is best at another time of day, plan accordingly. You will do better work and save time doing it.

43. Involve everyone in home tasks. When everyone pitches in, everyone benefits. Allow everybody to choose the job they prefer or do best.

44. Set time bites. Don't try to do it all at once. Instead, set aside short chunks of time. A rule of thumb is one-half hour per day going through clutter or trying to organize drawers. It took longer than that to make the clutter. Don't expect it to go away in a snap.

45. Find time for yourself. Even if it seems as if your jobs at work and home are never done, make certain that you find at least a half hour each day to yourself. You need it to renew your energy, to meditate and prepare for the day. Try getting up an hour earlier than anyone else in your house. Spend this time just doing what you want to do.

46. Consolidate your efforts. Keep your movements to a minimum. If you are cleaning, do one section at a time. If you are writing, complete the task before you move on to something else.

47. Duplicate errands. Don't run out to the post office, go home and then go to the dry cleaner. Plan the errands, decide where you will be and do them all at the same time.

48. Instant chores. Don't put off the routine chores. Do them at once. Do the dishes as soon as you've eaten. Make the bed as soon as you rise. Open the mail as soon as you get it and decide right then what you are going to do with it.

49. Use a timer. A timer can notify you that it is time for you to leave for an appointment when you are absorbed in a project. Need to limit a phone call? Set the timer. Need an hour to work on a specific task? Set the timer. It will help you control how much time you spend.

50. Give yourself a cushion. Set your personal deadlines a few days early to cover any problems that may arise. Leave for a meeting early enough so that you arrive at least 5 to 10 minutes early. This gives you time to relax for a few minutes and shows courtesy to your host. This will help you keep the stress to a minimum.

1. Put a check by the techniques in this chapter that you do not incorporate at home or at the office. Why? Go back over the checks and prioritize them according to your needs and goals.

2. Which of these techniques is the most unpleasant for you to follow through on? Make a conscious decision to add them to your working style first.

3. Declare vacation time for yourself everyday. Take one half hour daily just to relax and do anything you want other than work. Read, take a long walk or just lay on the floor and meditate.

4. Be gentle with yourself. Don't berate yourself for allowing the disorganization in the first place. Use the time instead to keep it that way.

Reflections

We hope that these suggestions will assist you in organizing your life. Your goal is to use time in the best ways that you can. You have to decide what works for you. Just remember that the greatest time-wasters are the ones that create stress and give you a false sense of urgency. Don't let yourself be fooled. No one gets everything in life, but we can all try to have everything that really matters. Being able to control how you use your time at home, within yourself and at the office will enable you to step back and make certain that you are still on track for what you want.

Don't get so trapped in running errands, doing tasks, keeping to your list and running faster and faster that you fail to take a few of the minutes that you've saved to reassess your life and your relationships. Time is what you make it. Be certain that you make it help you get things done in small, significant steps, leaving enough latitude for you to enjoy living.

INDEX

action plan 11
arguments 48-50
around-the-desk organization 33
authority vs. responsibility 55
avoid crises 70-71
avoid interruption 22-25, 67, 107
barriers to delegating 54-55
be considerate 44
be flexible 28, 106
be friendly 45
be practical 87
beware of TV 79
building relationships 45, 105
calendars 37, 83, 105
changing your behavior 93-94
communication 48-50
controlling the meeting 20-21
coupons and recipes 86
"co-workers role" 43
crisis time management 63-72
cut through clutter 66
deadline crisis 63-64
define the problem 48
delegate 54-56, 106

desktop organization 32-33, 107
determining the real issue 47
distractions 13-29, 58, 60
do it 67, 87, 106
drop-in visitors 24-25
effective delegating 56
evaluate 32
evening survival 78-79
explaining what needs to be done 43
external distractions 13-29
facing the day 74-77
file space 37
filing system 86, 108
five steps to completing tasks 66-67
get focused 66
get to know employees 45
getting started 69-70
give credit 44
goal setting 6-9, 105
"Golden Rule" 44
home organizing 81-90
impulse buying 88
incentives and rewards 44
inventory 34
involve everyone 74
least favorite jobs 83
limit trips 40
mail 86
maintain a calendar 37, 83, 105
make time for yourself 110
meeting reports 21-22
meetings 13-22
mind control 91-102
minimizing 107
negotiating deadlines 65

never enough time 59-60
office equipment 37-38, 106
organization 81-89
other perspectives 48
overlook outbursts 45
overwhelmed 59-60, 91-92
"pack rat" 87-88
paper pileup 39-40
paperwork at home 86
perfectionism 98-99, 107
personal reading file 40
phone directory 34-35, 108
point system 77-78
pre-meeting organization 14
prime time 100
priorities at home 10, 73-74
procrastination 97-98, 106
remain objective 47
schedule major projects 83
self-assessment 5-12, 92-94
set deadlines 82-83
setting priorities 10, 73-74, 105
spirit of cooperation 44
stress and conflict 92-93
study behavior patterns 48
style 96-97
subscriptions 40
system 86
TAF system 39-40, 86
take time to organize 106
telephone calls 22-24, 108
the organizer 38
time allocation 37
time frames and deadlines 44
time management 53-60, 63-72, 73-80

time planning for working parents 73-80
time enough 82-84
understanding priorities 5, 66
unmatched priorities 47
use lists 84, 105
using time 27-29
who attends meetings 19-20
working with others 43-51

Notes

Notes

Notes

Notes

Notes

Notes